4–

# THE OWL PAPERS

# THE OWL
# PAPERS

Jonathan Evan Maslow

Vintage Books
A Division of Random House
New York

FIRST VINTAGE BOOKS EDITION, October 1988

The lines by Ted Hughes on page 175 are from his poem
"My Grandpa."

Parts of the first chapter appeared in different form in *GEO*
magazine, © 1982 Knapp Communications Corporation.

**Library of Congress Cataloging-in-Publication Data**
Maslow, Jonathan Evan.
  The owl papers.
  Originally published: 1st ed. New York: Dutton, c1983.
1. Owls. I. Title.
QL696.S8M33 1988    598′.970973    87-45972
ISBN 0-394-75813-7 (pbk.)

DESIGNED AND ILLUSTRATED
BY MAURA FADDEN ROSENTHAL

Manufactured in the United States of America
10 9 8 7 6 5 4 3 2 1

For my uncle, Max Blatt

# CONTENTS

# WINTER

## The Duke of Pelham Bay

Is the owl a gentleman? Listen. Not far from where I live in
New York City is a place called Pelham Bay Park, marking
the city's northern limits. The name is something of a mis-
nomer, inasmuch as the "bay" is little more than a smear of
Long Island Sound that happens to run aground on a cren-
ulation of land. What's more, it's not exactly a park, either.
There is a picnic area, a golf course, and a beach, where in
the summer you can see the greatest collection of gangs,
geeks, and druggies New York has to offer. Yet for all this
there are sizable tracts of woods and wetlands that go un-
tended and largely unknown, all within view of the Empire
State Building. Largely deserted from Labor Day in September to Memorial Day weekend in May, the place is so mar-
ginal that a horde of homeless people have knocked together
a shantytown of crates and driftwood and live there in the
woods like gypsies, without anyone taking the least notice.

One winter, incarcerated in a dingy apartment by the
worst cold wave since 'aught-nine, and very much in need
of outdoor adventure, I happened to run across an intriguing
reference to the Great Horned Owl in John Bull's compen-
dious volume, *Birds of the New York Area*. Bull stated that
the Great Horned Owl, which the French once called *Le
Grand Duc* and I call the Duke or Duchess, "has in recent
years become more adapted to the metropolitan area, appearing on the outskirts of the larger towns, and often seen
in some of the larger city parks." The Duke's nest, Bull

continued, "has been found within the past few years in Bronx and Pelham Bay parks."

The Duke and Duchess of Pelham Bay Park: just the needed tonic for the big-city winter blues. I heaved map, gas-fueled hand-warmer, bird guide, binoculars, coffee thermos, pipe, tobacco rasher, lighter, penknife, pocket watch, flashlight, pen, and notebook into a daypack; donned long johns, ragg socks, jeans, flannel shirt, heavy sweater, wool scarf, wool babushka, mittens, and bright orange wool Kiwi shirt; and, having now prepared for an expedition to the North pole as much as the north Bronx, set off on a wheezing public bus across Fordham Road to Pelham Bay.

At the entrance to Split Rock Public Golf Course in Pelham Bay was a typed notice on a tidy stand, like the ones you see announcing the luncheon menu in fancy restaurant lobbies. It said: CLOSED FOR THE WINTER.

Two groundskeepers came out of the clubhouse, chunky, jolly men in heavy sweatshirts and workpants, speaking mellifluous Italian to each other as they stuffed oversize sandwiches into their mouths.

"Hi," I said. "Seen any owls around?"

They were not only friendly but knew exactly what I was talking about.

"Ahh, leetle one, beeg one," said the first, moving his hands like an accordion player.

"U-lu-lu-lu-lu-lu-lu!" sang the other, hunching his shoulders, flippering his hands, and rocking from side to side, in a marvelous imitation of a penguin.

"All the time here," the first groundsman assured me.

"Really? Where?"

"Here, you look." He marched straight for the very first inkberry bush planted beside the clubhouse, parted the branches, and, with a gesture worthy of a Florentine prince, invited me to peer in. The lower branches were heavily splattered with "whitewash," evidence of an excreting owl. Below on the ground were several owl pellets—the regurgitated remains of the indigestible parts of the owl's prey— little larger than cigarette butts. Also, slices of Jewish rye. I looked back at the sandwiches the men were carrying and, by matching bread types, deduced that they had been feeding the owl. Though, of course, owls being strictly carnivorous, it might be the salami they'd want, not the rye. From the look of things, they had a little Acadian, or Saw-whet, Owl roosting in the inkberries.

"Big one down there," said the other groundsman, waving in the direction of the fairway. "Huj-a-big-one."

This sounded more like the Duke or Duchess, since the Great Horned Owl is the heaviest and fiercest nocturnal raptor, or bird of prey, in North America—not likely to coop in a clubhouse shrub, or feed on rye bread, no matter how well adapted to metropolitan areas it might become.

"All right if I go out there?" I asked.

"Sure, oh sure, you go," agreed the jolly groundsman.

"Under the bridge, hole in the fence," added his mate. And with jaunty waves that reminded me of Herr Settembrini bidding Hans Castorp adieu as the latter set off to get lost in the snowstorm in *The Magic Mountain*, the two Italians climbed aboard their pickup truck and drove away.

There was a railroad bridge indeed, but no hole in the cyclone fence. I tossed my pack under, climbed over, and stood facing the unknown. The misty air filled my city lungs. The fairway rig swarmed with a thousand or more Canada geese, honking and bickering like a living black and white quilt spread over the ground as far as the eye could see. They greeted my arrival as they might have a gunshot. First a few lifted off, then more, until the entire flock was in agitated motion, crowding the sky. The racket of wings beating and horns honking lasted a long time. When it finally faded into the west, the only sound was the soft swish of cars speeding by on the Hutchinson parkway some distance away.

Exhilarated by near silence and the feel of the weather on my face, I moved through light ground fog to the pine groves, where I found pellets in the pine needles beneath the trees. Not small pellets, like the ones back at the clubhouse, but large pellets, as big as golf balls, which I also found there. But more pellets than golf balls. Five, ten, a dozen, more. Gray, hairy, wet, tightly balled masses, with delicate white bones protruding. Fresh pellets indicate owlish presence.

I had my eyes glued so tightly to the ground that only peripheral vision clued me in to the fact that a shadow was passing over my head. When I raised my eyes, it was in time to catch only a glimpse of an enormous, dark-colored bird stealing away like a specter, already a hundred yards off. A glimpse—fleeting one, at that—and the bird vanished into the leafless trees on the far side of the fairway. It could have been a hawk or a crow: with no positive ID, I couldn't be sure. But from all the owl signs under the pines, I'd have staked my life it was the Duke or Duchess. Why else would the adrenaline be pumping through my veins?

I quickly stuffed three pellets into my pack for later investigation, and gave chase. Now began a game of hide and seek: me dashing over the fairways scanning the distant tree-lines, the bird never waiting for me to get anywhere close, revealing its presence only by its departure, keeping a line of trees between us at all times. All I could make out was a quick flit at the paltry limit of human vision, giant wings disappearing at the precise moment of being noticed as the bird slipped into some farther grove. Puffing, I raced after it, hardly knowing my bearings and not caring, tripping because my eyes were focused on the far purlieus for a shape, a movement, anything. On and on we chased, the bird leading its pursuer over hill and down dale, effortlessly flaunting its power to fly, to make itself one with the winter woods. How well this bird knew its territory. How easily it toyed with the earthbound stranger. I had no real hope of catching up. I couldn't even spot the creature until it moved once more. Deeper and deeper into the reaches of the park it eluded me. I was coming to realize that running across open terrain in full view of a bird of prey with eyesight ten—no, a hundred—times better than mine would accomplish exactly nothing. I was also coming to realize I was lost. Suddenly I pulled up short, my mouth went dry, and the hair stood stiff on the nape of my neck. Ahead, no more than a hundred feet away, were three wild dogs.

Actually, feral, not wild, would be the better term, for these dogs must have been born *domesticus* and escaped—or been abandoned, as often happens when city dwellers take on pets they can't care for. They appeared to be mean and vicious curs: it had been a long time since any of them had worn a collar or eaten from a bowl. They were sulking in some tall phragmites, sniffing the air with lowered heads, and curling their upper lips so that yellow fangs showed, though they weren't growling—not yet. I suppose the dogs were as startled at my sudden intrusion on their resting place as I was by their sudden appearance in front of me. They watched me, lips quivering. We'd happened upon each other too close to pretend we weren't there. So we stared at each other rather dumbly, trying to remember a million years of evolution, what went before this and what was supposed to happen next.

No—no! I wanted to shout. This is all a big mistake. It

was the Great Horned Owl I was after, not you. Why, I love dogs. Always have. Had them since I was a kid. Drop by the house for some Alpo, any time!

Where were my Settembrinis now?

I considered screaming, but who would hear? And if anyone heard, who would come to my aid? Unlike birds, it suddenly struck me, we humans have no instinctive alarm cries to set off equally instinctive swarming-to-assistance responses. "Help!" I might have yelled, but what if the sound reached only drivers hurtling down the distant highways at sixty miles per hour? Even if they could hear me, nothing in their genetic code would make them stop; it would take a conscious decision, a sense of ethics!

My imagination was running now. If the dogs attacked successfully, I envisioned my corpse rotting in Pelham Bay Park for days before the groundskeepers spotted the body, minus the rump steaks. I even saw the obligatory headline in the tabloids: MANHATTAN MAN FOUND IN WEIRD BRONX RITUAL MURDER.

Little would they know that the only cult I belonged to was the National Audubon Society.

Meanwhile, the situation was not getting any less precarious. I watched the dogs, they watched me. They were not making any movement toward me, I noticed. Perhaps because they were equally fearful, or from some respect for humans, latent in their jackal genes. From somewhere, I recalled that a wild dog won't normally attack a man, one on one. But if you run, and they give chase, pack behavior takes over. Once the leader of the pack sinks his teeth in your flesh, it's over.

This gave me small comfort. Like our distant ancestors' on the African plains, my eyes searched for any possible escape route. If I dropped everything and hightailed it, I

figured no more than a forty—sixty chance of making it to
the chain-link fence, all the way back across the golf course,
before they did any severe damage. Not a good option.

The dogs, as I said, were thin and hungry looking, but
they did have rugged, thick winter coats, no doubt the result
of healthy outdoor living. One could admire that. At least
they were not human playthings, led out at eight and six to
relieve themselves on fire hydrants. They had repossessed
some of their canine dignity. My eyes met the eyes of the
small pack's leader, a heavy, white shepherd type. I thought
I caught in his look the slightest movement away from me—
nothing so definitive as a tail wag or head toss, mind you,
only the merest break in our mutual stare. Not even that.
Perhaps nothing more than the subtle suggestion in his eyes
that if I looked away for a moment, he would look away for
a moment, too. Once we had the momentum of disarma-
ment going, maybe we could find a way out of this predic-
ament without either of us losing face. It was worth a shot.

I dropped my eyes, and followed up the gesture by taking
one small, slow step backward, then another, until my foot
lodged against a stick. It was dry and hard, nicely knobbed
at the end like a club. I bent down very slowly and grasped
it in my hand. This seemed a prudent defense measure.
Holding the stick well out in front of my face, so the dogs
could clearly see it, I continued my cautious retreat. The
dogs sniffed the air, snarled, but finally decided it wasn't
worth it: they made no motion to follow. In another minute
I was racing back across the fairway as fast as my legs could
carry me. I didn't stop running till I reached the clubhouse.

Enough excitement for one day. The owl had displayed
superior powers and evaded me with a nonchalance that was
absolute, almost contemptuous. I'd nearly been wiped out
by wild dogs. Round one to the Duke or Duchess: my self-

esteem had been taken down several notches, but in its place grew an understanding of human limitations, always a good lesson for a budding naturalist. When I reached my apartment building and saw the yellow taxis in the street, the doorman out front kibbitzing with his cronies, the elderly ladies wheeling their shopping carts into the elevator, I felt as if I'd spent the day on the dark side of the moon.

In his eighteenth-century masterpiece *The Natural History of Selbourne*, the British country parson and naturalist Gilbert White dispensed the following wisdom: "Men that undertake only one district are much more likely to advance natural knowledge than those that grasp at more than they can possibly be acquainted with." White's own method of research was simplicity itself: each day, he took a long walk and noted down precisely what he observed. No contemporaneous biography of the shy curate remains, but we do know that he could often be seen standing where the fields bordered the woods, marking the list of birds he always carried in his pocket: "I noted each day the continuance or omission of each bird's song, so that I am as sure of the certainty of my facts as a man can be of any transaction whatever."

In more than fifty years of walking and jotting, this inspired provincial pastor rarely strayed beyond the meadows and hedgerows of his beloved Selbourne parish. Yet White's keen observations virtually transformed the study of nature, which, following the great systematizer Linnaeus, had previously been devoted mainly to classifying collections of dead animal skins, dried flowers, and pinned butterflies. By concentrating on what was local and alive, Gilbert White performed two magnificent services for the generations of naturalists to come. First, he pioneered what has come to be known as "fieldwork," where conclusions are deduced from actual observation. And second, maybe more importantly, he launched the eminently democratic notion that the secrets of creation are equally available to the squire and the common man—to whomever takes the time and trouble to observe nature closely.

What held true of White's method then holds true today, when the most important work for naturalists, professional and amateur alike, is as much the preservation of life forms as the discovery of natural processes. To know the owls, class Aves, order Strigiformes, you don't need a degree from Cornell or a grant from Exxon. You needn't go on exotic safaris or buy a lot of expensive gadgets. Only pay heed to whatever district you live in, and listen to the night surrounding you: there's more going on under your own window than you can absorb in a full and fruitful lifetime.

It was indeed outside my bedroom window that this preoccupation with owls first took shape many years ago. As a child, I'd lie in bed at night, listening to spring's nocturne. A rhythm of crickets and peepers. The bass solos of bullfrogs. The wailing of lovesick cats. A particularly vain mockingbird with a seemingly endless repertoire, who would perch on the streetlamp like a young Caruso and sing for hours without repeating a single passage. Only gradually did I pick out from this harmony an unfamiliar, gently trilling hoot, as if a wood nymph were shivering slightly in the chilly night. A long, unbroken, understated note, slowly descending, quite reedy or hollow. While other voices proclaimed, this one seemed to pose the question, "Who are you?" It was the same question that ancient heroes heard from within when they stood facing dragons.

In time I came to anticipate the owl's comforting lament. It served as a lullaby, song and sign from Mother Nature that all was well with the world and would remain so till morning. Yet there was a certain mystery in that tranquil zephyr of voice. For at first I'd hear it close by the window, then quickly off to the south, next just as far off to the east, then close by again. This bird seemed to be everywhere at once. How, I wondered, did it accomplish this feat?

I concocted three explanations for the phenomenon. Either (a) there was more than one owl out there, hooting at each other; or (b) there was just one owl, a ventriloquist; or else (c) the owl was not constrained by time and space like the rest of us, but had the sprite's capacity to be here, there, and everywhere, all at once. Out the window I climbed one night to find out: my first field expedition.

Outside I entered a new world, as lush with foreign smells and strange music as an Arab market. Our house stood at the margin of a recent suburban development, where the terrain dropped off into a swampy wood of emaciated, interlaced maples with a stagnant stream creeping through. By day, there were mud carp in the stream, and muskrats holing up in the red clay banks. There were green garter snakes slithering through the grasses, and an occasional water moccasin, which we called "cottonmouth" and scrupulously avoided. Cardinals, robins, and bluejays camped in the foliage, rabbits burrowed in the catbriers. When nights turned frosty at harvest moon, meadow mice retreated into our basement. If you got out by first light, your eyes were treated to the ennobling sight of ring-necked pheasants, dawn dandies, performing a stately pavane up the neighborhood lawns. Or a furtive red fox, dashing for cover after a night of pillage in the outlying poultry farms.

All these creatures were familiar under the sun, but the night brewed different intoxicants. The unseen ground was chill and wet underfoot, the air laced with sweet perfumes. I could hear the sibilant leaves overhead, and the aged weeping willow tree, groaning its infirmity by the brook. The sudden plops in the marshy muck, and the swift zing of insects grazing my ears. But above all, as I tiptoed forward, listening hard over the beating of my heart, I could hear the unidentifiable creepings of the small night creatures, the edgy crunching of leaves, the achingly slow scrunching through brush, the cautious, labored steps: the steps of lives lived in utter fear, ever on the brink of sudden obliteration, and wise to it. There were fantastic battles and subterfuges going on out there, strategies and maneuvers the mere fact of darkness kept hidden from me. I was tantalized by the expectation that something important—a matter of life and death—was about to happen. I was also blind and clumsy. Unadapted to this shadowy world, I felt a bit vulnerable, too, and envious of any creature that could master this elemental state, the night.

Eventually, I located the trilling owl, who wasn't the least shy, perched in one of those swamp maples that have one fat foot fixed firmly on the ground and half a dozen gracile arms. Wonder of wonders: the longer I waited, the more my eyes grew accustomed, and the better I began to see. The night is never really as dark as you think. There's always some moonbeams, a touch of starlight, or only that narrow hatband of faint luminosity at the horizon called zodiacal light—in the west, the memory of a day that will never come again; in the east, the promise of a new one. Gradually, the owl changed, from a small, undifferentiated blob to a little gray creature with a spoon face and ears that went off sideways at a crazy angle, like the flat hat of a proper bourgeois in a Rembrandt portrait. Its head was tucked deeply into its shoulders, the way one imagines Napoleon posed the night before Waterloo.

I raced back inside the house and emerged again with a flashlight, thereby rediscovering an important boon to owlers—that owls do not seem to associate a flashlight with danger. My owl showed no alarm but continued to rotate its head in robotic twists. Now I could see the huge eyes, shining red as glowing coals, and the sharp, hooked beak, which looked so much like a nose. I was completely transfixed: the bird looked human. Its face seemed to possess not merely acute intelligence but a bluff expression of utter confidence. A potentate in epauletted greatcoat, all of eight inches tall.

My curiosity aroused, next morning I consulted a small bird manual we happened to have around the house called, simply, *Birds*. There I learned that my owl was a Screech Owl, a name borrowed from a European relative. (Even then the name struck me as totally inappropriate, since I never heard the little guy come out with anything vaguely approaching a screech.) I also learned from the guide that "keen eyesight and noiseless flight" enable the Screech Owl "to prey on field rodents." (So field rodents were the makers of all those anxious scrunchings!) And that "this owl is found in two color phases: a gray and a reddish brown."

"Noiseless flight." "Color phases." "Bird of prey." These words had an intoxicating effect, but I had come no closer to an explanation of the mysterious movable voice. I kept vigil for my Screech Owl from then on, but could never manage to see the bird fly to or from its favorite perch in the swamp maples. The owl would turn up there frequently but not regularly. Often it would appear just at dusk, as if out of nothingness. Look once, there was a stump of gray bark. Look again, there was Screech Owl, looking devilishly pleased at its now-you-see-me act. The owl's ditty continued to quiver from near and far. So it was a long time before I was disabused of hypothesis (c), the sprite. I knew my first owl as a grand master of concealment, appearing and disappearing at will, making its voice dance over darkness, wooing the listener out into the freedom of night. It seems I was already well on the way to becoming an owler—one of that band of ornithological fanatics who have fallen under the owl's spell. Of course, a more mature inquiry into the wandering hoot would have proved the correct answer was (b), the ventriloquist. Owls can adjust the size of the air passage in their vocal chords, shrewdly disguising their voices to avoid being located and attacked by an enemy—gobbled down, for instance, by a larger owl.

# F O U R

Seeking a spot of indoor work before returning to Pelham Bay, I went to the American Museum of Natural History to see the owls. They were in a glass case in a small nook off to the side of Luis Agassiz Fuertes's colorful mural of a flamingo colony in the Bahamas. It did seem better in the Bahamas: standing on the purest of white beaches, under the clearest of azure skies, the voluptuous, long-legged pink waders made the owls seem dowdy and dry. The owls could not get over the affront. They perched with wide, morbid stares, condemned for all time to watch the cheerful tropical tableau next door. Oooh, they seemed to say, if only we could break out of stuffed reality into that delicate mass of roseate flesh. Thrash the pinkos, waste the nests, guzzle down the warm, wet eggs, and take no prisoners. What mischief we could do!

The taxidermist's art is all in getting a lifelike pose. Here, they'd succeeded. There was nothing cute or cuddly about the fourteen species of North American nocturnal birds of prey on display. The Barn Owl, *Tyto alba*, hunches over, snickering, a greedy ghoul. The Great Gray Owl, *Strix nebulosa*, is enormous—and enormously sad and world-weary, its facial disks a network of worry lines in dark, concentric rings. The small Saw-whet Owl, *Aegolius acadicus*, stands with its back toward us, its head swiveled 180 degrees to smite the onlooker, demonstrating the ability of owls to rotate their heads on extremely flexible necks—which, by the way, contain seven additional vertebrae for precisely this purpose. Impressive is the Snowy Owl, *Nyctea scandiaca*, with its sleek suit of pure white and dark chocolate barring, its elegant white face and white furry feet, a flying snowstorm from the Arctic. The homeliest owl was also the tiniest: the Pygmy Owl, *Glaucidium gnoma*, no larger than a paunchy sparrow, with bulging, goitered eyes, its coat mousedun with white splotches stuck on haphazardly, in no definite design or pattern. But without question the most awesome was the Great Horned Owl, *Bubo virginianus*, all its power deftly hidden behind rows and rows of somber plumes, ending finally in fully splayed talons, black meat hooks.

And the prettiest owl? That would be a contest I would not want to judge. Owls are not flashy dressers. For beauty, they don't compare to the flamingo, the quetzal, the peacock. They are plumed like the practical, conservative executives of night they are. They scoff at the frivolity of birds who waste precious energy on sexual adornment. Once the lights are off, says the owl, who cares? Yet I admire the way their markings show such variation using so few colors. Working only in umber, buff, pearl, clove, and soot, nature has done a great deal. This variety of contours, the zigzag lines and wavy lines, the rows of dots and streaks, the stripes and bars, the speckling, and the toupees of polka dots: it is as if a Chinese calligrapher had stroked and dabbed, showing all that can be accomplished with only line and dot. In the sterile glass case, the patterns were visible. But the same patterns in the field and forest will blend perfectly against their background, utilitarian camouflage for birds that must sleep by day and survive.

"Owls have always had a considerable fascination for mankind," the legend under the owl case informs us. "By day they usually sit quietly in a thick evergreen, but at night their sonorous hooting reveals their presence."

Just then, a mother came by, leading her small daughter by the hand. "Look," she said to the child. "Look at all the different kinds of owls.

"Ooooooooh," cooed the little girl. But then, suddenly perceiving something ominous in the Duke's bent stare, the child's innocent face registered horror, and she grasped tightly at her mother's hand. "I don't like them, Mommy."

"Okay," said Mommy. "Let's go look at the pretty pink flamingos."

Because they have always carried the mysteries of night with them, owls are less known than other birds. And because the unknown is fearful, owls have historically been less loved, too: " 'Twas the owl that shrieked the fatal bellman, which gives the stern'st good night," said Lady Macbeth, taking the bird of night's doleful hoot as tidings that her traitorous husband had murdered his king. Shakespeare was borrowing freely from an ancient superstition that the owl's screech announces death. The Roman histories tell us that no fewer than three Caesars had their deaths foretold by the dire hooting of owls during daylight. Julius Caesar was one, the Emperor Augustus another. Commodus Aurelius took a meeting with a Screech Owl in his chambers on the day of his demise. When Agrippa, Roman usurper of the Hebrew throne, noticed an Eagle Owl perched on a cord over his throne in Caesarea, he gasped and promptly fell back in a fatal swoon, an early example of self-fulfilling prophecy. The Latin word for owl, *Bubo*, derives from the low-pitched hoo-hoo of the Horned Owl, and was customarily preceded by the epithet *sinister* or *infestus*, meaning "dangerous" or "hostile." According to Pliny the Elder, the Roman natural historian who never spent much time in the field (and cribbed from Plato, to boot), "the owl betokeneth always some heavy news and is most execrable and accursed in presaging public affairs. . . . If he be seen either within cities or abroad in any place, it is not for good, but prognosticates some fearful misfortune."

The Romans held dreadful beliefs about owls, and avoided nocturnal raptors whenever possible. Once, at the beginning of the consulship, a Horned Owl had the temerity to fly straight into the Capitol during working hours. Immediately, the Senate ordered the priests to perform a general lustration, or purification ceremony, as the poet Hudibras wrote, "The round faced prodigy to avert, from doing town or country hurt." It is curious that the bird the Romans stigmatized as death's messenger usually seems to have arrived at a moment when the Romans themselves were conspiring evil. This, however, could be practically any time, for the Romans were not particularly sweet-natured, nor their consciences spotless, nor their hands free of innocent blood. The Roman emperors chose the eagle as their mighty emblem: perhaps they found *Bubo* too reminiscent of their darker lusts.

In any case, the Romans left an indelible mark on the way later centuries viewed the owl. From the earliest days of the Catholic Church, Christian folklore took up where Roman superstition left off, derogating the image of the owl even further. The owl was a sweet singer, one Christian legend said, until it witnessed the crucifixion. Then the owl's voice turned dour, and it sought the shadows evermore. There was, too, the strange tale about Christ and the baker's daughter, which persisted in Europe right up until the last century. It seems Jesus once asked a baker's wife for bread. She put a large loaf in the oven to bake, but her daughter secretly reduced the dough to a very small size. However, the tiny loaf suddenly swelled to enormous size, and the astonished daughter cried out, "Heugh, heugh, heugh!" Christ punished her by transforming her into an owl. Perhaps the story warns women to leave things as they are: tamper with the status quo, and you'll spend eternity as the freakish bird.

As Manichaean symbol of evil, the owl was persecuted into the Dark Ages. While feudal princes made a fine art of warfare and exploitation, it was the owl, the goat, and the monkey, which were portrayed together as the unholy trio, anticlerical and anti-establishment. A twelfth-century bestiary taught that, because owls fly at night, they "represent the Jews, who refuse redemption. They love darkness more than [the] light of Christ." Medieval children were frightened into obedience with a couplet that told them the price of misbehavior and rebellion:

> *Oh——o—o—o——o!*
> *I once was a king's daughter and sat on my father's knee*
> *But now I'm a poor hoolet, and hide in a hollow tree!*

Again, when the ghastly flames of the Inquisition burned hottest in Spain, the story was current that Satan himself kept an owl for a pet. What heretic, wizard, sorcerer, or witch was not consort and colleague of the gruesome owl?

This deep-seated tradition of associating a bird of eccentric habits and disagreeable voice with evil and dread endured with astonishing tenacity into enlightened times—only now with the pretext that owls damaged livestock and game. The Marquess of Bute, for example, required his gamekeepers to swear an oath, ending with the words, "And finally I shall use my best endeavour to destroy all birds of prey with their nests, so help me God." American ranchers on the western frontier, who slaughtered Indian and buffalo alike in the name of progress, also had their unholy trio. Its members were the wolf, the bear, and the Great Horned Owl. Accused of willful savagery in the killing of livestock, *Bubo* became a varmint, and had a bounty placed on its head. Little sleep was lost if a shot owl turned out to be some entirely different species. Across the United States, eliminating owls was not only tolerated but actually considered in the public interest and legitimized by naturalists, who, by this time, should certainly have known better. Consider the account of Neltje Blanchen, an influential turn-of-the-century ornithologist, whose 1898 portrait of the Great Horned Owl resonates with Romanesque loathing and bristles with medieval rhetoric. *Bubo virginianus*, Blanchen states,

> does more damage than all other species put together. . . . his ponderous body gives him impressive size and power, earned through constant exercise of savage instincts. No one ever finds this hunter in poor condition; diligent and overpowering in the chase, he feasts where others starve, bringing down upon the innocent heads of several members of his tribe the punishment of sins of his commission by undiscriminating farmers. . . . Not until dusk, with uncanny silence and hawklike swiftness, he begins his nefarious work . . . chickens, ducks, geese, turkeys, pigeons on the farm will be decapitated if too large to eat entire, for the brains of the victim are the tidbits the executioner delights in.

It is only ten years since dwindling American owl populations finally received federal protection. But as conservation authorities are well aware, owls are still shot on sight in many rural areas, the thanks they receive for keeping grain-bins and barns free of rodents.

Perhaps the last refuge of the owl's old sinister reputation is in contemporary films. Whenever a character is wandering the woods alone at night, courting some ghoulish disaster, the obligatory sound effect is the hooting of the Great

Horned Owl. It's remarkable how the owl's voice still announces menace in an age when most moviegoers have never even seen a live owl outside a zoo. Owlers watch these movie scenes with skepticism. Not long ago, I saw one horror film in which a Horned Owl's voice bayed in the spooky woods, while the camera showed a Screech Owl. But I suppose that's Hollywood.

Through the ages, we've projected this profound sense of foreboding onto the owl and drafted the bird into our deepest fears. Why? Perhaps only because the owl controls the province of night, repository of our irrational selves. We would rather deny that darkness within us, waiting to burst out whenever reason sleeps.

It was once stated by an anonymous demographer that every person in the United States lives within twenty-five miles of some owl's territory. I don't know how he came up with the statistic, since nocturnal birds of prey don't lend themselves to census techniques especially well. Nevertheless, the best way to find an owl is to first locate the bird's winter roost. Once an owl finds a dark, quiet, secure, secluded spot to sleep during the daylight hours, it will usually make a habit of returning there, often for the entire season—sometimes year after year. Mainly, owls go for the conifer trees, where the dense needles provide excellent cover.

Locating roosts is relatively easy, because owls provide such good clues. Owls are fast eaters. They don't waste time stripping the meat from the bones. They don't chew twenty times before swallowing. One gulp, or two, and they bolt the prey item right down. But the owl's digestive system isn't equipped with strainers, jigsaws, or rotary blades, so later the owl casts up that furry, gray pellet. Usually, owls toss a pellet on territory to lighten their hunting weight before the night's action commences. A second pellet normally is dropped back at the roost, and the pellets collect under the trees. In winter, particularly when there's snow on the ground, pellets under the pines are dead giveaways that the owl is close by. If you visit the spot regularly, you can get a fair idea of the number of squeakers the owl has done in during a given period. Unless, that is, the owls have been

roosting there so long that it's no longer possible to distin-
guish recent pellets from ancient ones. Gilbert White had a
friend, "a gentleman of the country of Wilts," who went out
"grubbing a vast hollow pollard-ash that had been the man-
sion of owls for centuries." At the bottom the gentleman
came upon "a congeries of bones of mice that had been
heaping together for ages." He reported, "there were bushels
of this kind of substance."

On my next visit to Pelham Bay Park, I located that Great
Horned's daytime roost. It was in a grove of gigantic hemlock trees at the very tip of Hunter's Island—which is not at
all an island, being connected to the rest of the park by a
thin neck of land. Like most owl roosts, this one was a
completely unappealing and slovenly site, full of broken
stumps, dead branches, and the rotting remnants of owl
gorges, fur and feathers and the dismembered parts of unfin-
ished feasts all about, not to mention the owl's indelicate,
defecatory "splash," slapped across the trunks and needles
like a coat of cheap whitewash. I counted over a hundred
pellets in that single area; not a bad winter's work.

I collected a few of the pellets, took them home, soaked
them separately overnight in lukewarm water, and then
pulled each pellet apart with tweezers, spreading the bones
out to classify them and mounting the results on poster
board. It took hours and hours to do this, which may thus
be categorized a "fascinating hobby." Most of the delicate
white bones of the owl pellet are easy to recognize, by shape
if not by species. The skulls are, of course, the most obvious. The mandible, or jawbone, is a heavyish hook, with a
row of smooth molars and one sharp incisor. The straight
bone knobbed at both ends, that's a humerus or possibly a
femur. The one shaped like a stirrup is the os coxae. The
wishbone-shaped one has a very thin bone on one side, the

fibula, and a thicker bone on the other side, the tibia. Pentagonal bones with open centers are vertebrae. When you find two, three, or even more skulls in the same pellet, you know that the owl is eating well. You get some idea of what efficient hunters they are. If you know rodent anatomy, you can precisely reconstruct the bird's diet.

Nevertheless, the skeletons found in owl pellets are usually incomplete. Sometimes there are more skulls than mandibles, sometimes more mandibles than skulls. Sometimes there are ten humeruses but only eight femurs. It's the accurate bone count that's the key to reading the future in owl pellets, but don't bother. Owl pellets are the most useless oracles ever known. No matter which way you dissect and mount them, owl pellets all predict the same thing: the fall of the Roman Empire.

# S  E  V  E  N

Beside the road in Pelham Bay Park, I spied a row of tall, venerable Eastern pines, standing deep in brambles. There were seven pines in all, planted in a neat row, as if someone had once begun a pine plantation but given up after the first row. I made for them to check for pellets, but had only reached the first tree when a Great Horned Owl came cruising past, blunt profile floating fast, followed by half a dozen crows in hot pursuit. The owl wheeled and came to rest high in the pines, and the crows landed all around it. It was barely first light, and the birds' black silhouettes were set against brightening sky. The owl perched stolidly, the skulking crows surrounding it adding an ominous, professional mood to the proceedings. The owl looked to be encircled by six cloaked hitmen, already at work in the early dawn, still groggy and fulfilling a contract without enthusiasm.

I backtracked to the road and sat on a black rock where I could watch without being noticed. I didn't have long to wait. Crows were arriving from every direction, now putting up a terrific racket of caws. The owl swooped out again, this time tailed by half a hundred crows. Shooting through the trees, the Great Horned landed in the crotch of a tall plane tree. Instantly, the crows were there, too. Now that the owl had perched again, even more crows flocked to harass it. Poor owl, I thought. Its night shift done, the bird probably wanted nothing more than a quiet place to nap, a good leav-

ing alone. Instead, a hundred outraged crows were there to
annoy it. What a life! But when I trained my glasses on the
owl, I noticed that the bird didn't appear the least perturbed.
A big Great Horned, probably a Duchess, she was calmly
rotating her head and blinking her eyes, while the crows
reached an advanced state of pandemonium. The crows kept
coming from every direction, each adding its angry, rasping
"aarrgh! aarrgh!" to the choral plaint—though none actually
tried to attack. The owl sat in the midst of this botheration
for a good ten minutes, oblivious or unmoved. Then, when
she was good and ready, the Duchess launched from her
perch, quickly hopped into the thick cover of a nearby hemlock—and completely vanished from view. The stunned
crows remained for a few more minutes, their yells gradually
subsiding into bickering, then slowly dispersed, a few at a
time, until one last crow stood shrieking in the hemlock.

Crows are obsessed with owls and practically make a pro-
fession of chasing them around. If you want to find owls but
can't locate pellets, the next best thing is to follow the crows.
They will lead you to the owls. Why crows mob owls probably has to do with a defensive flocking instinct, set off by
visual recognition of a predator's shape. But crows are such
highly intelligent birds it often seems they are acting out a
social ritual, the envy of the lowly scavenger for the vaunted
bird of prey. In the spring, a variety of passerine species will
sometimes form such a posse and try to oust an owl from
their vicinity. Songbirds, too, seem to respond to the threat
signaled by the predator's shape, but the medieval author of
"The Owl and the Nightingale," who was the first to dub
this response "mobbing," blamed the owl in moral terms:

*I know how cruelly you attack*
*Small birds who cannot fight you back;*

*At every opportunity*
*You peck and tear them wantonly.*
*And that is why all birds detest you,*
*Why when they find you they molest you,*
*Screeching and crying as they chase*
*And mob you till you leave the place.*

The next Pelham Bay owl to surface turned out to be an emergency-room job rushed crosstown to a Brooklyn bird hospital run by one of the city's two licensed bird rehabilitators, Hanna Richard. I never actually got to see it—the owl died before I could get out to Brooklyn, delayed by a blizzard that knocked out the subways and shut the city down. When I arrived at the cozy waterfront bungalow, the snow was still falling in thick, silent sheets of sugar flakes. Inside, warm yellow lights brightened color photographs of owls in the living room. The sideboard was full of owl bric-a-brac, those little porcelain figures sentimentalists collect. Hanna, a petite, German-born, blond woman, who looks ten years younger than her actual forty, was grieving over the owl's death. She was like a doctor who'd just lost a patient. Sinking behind a mug of coffee in the living room also inhabited by a live Screech Owl, a Saw-whet Owl, and a mending merlin falcon in a wire cage, Hanna said, in a soft and tiny voice, "We can't save them all. There are so many injured birds. Look, we just do everything we can. He was such a beautiful little fella, too, our Barn Owl. You should have seen him. We'd already named him Tyto."

It helped to talk about it.

Slowly, the details of the incident emerged from our conversation. Forty-eight hours before, Hanna had received a call from a Bronx couple who'd picked up the injured Barn Owl on the road in Pelham Bay Park. The bird was crippled and couldn't fly. After telephoning Hanna, the couple gave the owl to the police, who raced it to Brooklyn in a squad car. Hanna examined the patient by hand, as she was trained to do in a long apprenticeship. Tyto was in poor shape. It couldn't lift its wings. Probable crushed spine below the fourteenth vertebra. The problem for bird rehabilitators is finding competent veterinarians to operate. In fact, the problem is finding any veterinarian to operate. Not when New York vets can rake in major dollars putting Park Avenue cats and dogs on diets. There's no money in bird surgery. Everything Hanna Richard does comes out of her own pocket—and out of her own heart, as big as all New York. Nevertheless, resourceful Hanna persuaded one of the few ornithological surgeons in the city, who works out of the Bronx Zoo, to operate on Tyto. The surgery lasted four hours. It went all right, though the prognosis was that the owl, if it survived, would probably remain crippled for life, never able to return to its habitat. But the owl didn't pull through. When it woke, Hanna gave it massive doses of Vitamin $B_1$, and fed it by tube. But the bird's stool became green and viscid. Twenty-four hours later, Tyto gave up the ghost.

I asked Hanna if she could say how the injury occurred.

"Well, at first, when I heard about it, I thought it must be a gunshot wound," she said. "We get a lot of those. There are so many morons running around New York with guns, you wouldn't believe it. But when I examined the little fella, I didn't find any flesh wounds, or shotgun pellets, which you'd expect. It's possible he may have crashed into a bus or got hit by a car. That happens all the time, too. Owls are supposed to be wise, but they're not, in human terms. They're poor, beautiful, dumb animals, who don't know that speeding cars are dangerous. But I don't think it was an accident, either. You know, a lot of bird rehabilitation is informed guesswork. Something about the way Tyto was injured, the broken vertebra, makes me think he was an attack victim."

But what predator could conceivably have been so bold as to attack a healthy, adult Barn Owl, one of nature's most adept hunters?

"Only thing I can think of," said Hanna Richard, "is a Great Horned Owl."

The Portuguese have a proverb that fits the Great Horned Owl to perfection. It goes: *En casa du Duque, não pasa fome.* Roughly translated, it means no one goes hungry at a Duke's house. The Great Horned Owl has never been accused of sitting on the groceries, nor of a lackadaisical attitude toward hunting. On the contrary, the Duke and Duchess have been accused of positively glorying in the kill and have long held a reputation as the "winged tigers" of the forest. Along with the owl's strange propensity for hooting in the dark comes its image as one of nature's consummate killers, which at times goes beyond mere subsistence to what some scientists label "food lust."

Here is a partial list of items in the Great Horned Owl's diet, drawn up by the early twentieth-century authority on the food of hawks and owls, Dr. A. K. Fisher, after dissecting some hundreds of owl stomachs:

three species of rabbits ("Undoubtedly, rabbits are its favorite food," observed Dr. Fisher)
cotton rat
two species of pocket gopher
two species of wood rat
chipmunk
two species of grasshopper mice
white-footed mouse
common rat
two species of ground squirrel

musk rat
fox squirrel
five species of meadow mice
short-tailed shrew
house mouse
flying squirrel
common shrew
kangaroo rat
scorpions
crawfish

Add to this list any bottom-feeding fish, for the Great
Horned Owl is sometimes seen wading in shallow water,
and not to wash its toes. Add also the common flicker,
blackbird, partridge, in fact any delectable bird. Add prairie
dog. Add woodchuck. Add rattlesnake, which the Great
Horned has been photographed subduing and consuming
simultaneously. By all means add the smaller owls—the
Screech Owl and the Barn Owl. And especially add skunk.
Horned owls seem to love a nice, fresh, smelly skunk; they
are one of the few predators that will go near it. Still, the
menu is incomplete. Some observers believe the number
of species taken and consumed by the Great Horned Owl
goes well over a hundred, and is really limited only by a
potential prey's size and availability. In its prime, an owl will
catch as many rodents in a night's work as a dozen cats.

Owls do have gigantic appetites, but generally speaking,
the bird of prey either bolts the prey entirely, eats the parts
it likes best and leaves the rest, or, if it has young to feed,
stockpiles surplus kill at the nest, the way a housewife might
fill her larder. Unlike men, no owl to anyone's knowledge
has ever died of gluttony—though owlets have been known
to consume their own siblings in their mad and constant
hunger.

Each autumn as the nesting season winds down, owls conclude their family business by driving their fledged young off the breeding grounds. Then the Great Horned mates part company, too, going separate ways to return to the life they are best suited for, the life of the solitary hunter. For the next several months, as though the advent of cold weather and short days triggers a biochemical change, the Duke and Duchess singlemindedly pursue their lonely task: hunting and eating, eating and hunting. By year's end, the predatory instinct has suppressed all others. Romance, play, and cooperation are better left for the summer season.

As this solitary hunting passion comes to the fore, the owl tunes its physical skills like any athletic virtuoso. And within a short period, the Great Horned Owl has become all but omnipotent in its several square miles of hunting territory. The owl has by this time also become a predator of opportunity, and will attack anything it has a decent chance of subduing. Any bird of prey naturally takes higher numbers of those prey species whose populations have grown large, or those that threaten to get out of control and are thus most readily available. Though it's nearly impossible to count a rodent population in any given area with accuracy, everyone knows rodents' outstanding traits: they eat everything in sight and reproduce incessantly. Presumably, rodent populations continually approach the upper limit of a habitat's ability to support them. The owl does not select any particular prey species to crop—the law of averages takes care of that. Nor does the owl entirely eliminate any species. What the owl does is prune, limit, regulate. So the owl's predation can in no sense be viewed as savage or brutal. An individual animal dies so that all others—including the prey's own species—can live. If the owl took a holiday, then overcrowding and extinction would inevitably follow. Instead, the owl leaves the diverse population of small mammals in better balance with the available food resources and with the other animals competing for that food. The owl is the chosen instrument of nature's controlled flux.

Ever since humans began to stop seeing Satan in every owl—a change that began in earnest only around the turn of the twentieth century—a good deal of scientific effort has gone into discovering how owls hunt with such excellent results in pitch darkness, night after night. While practical considerations make field studies of hunting owls rare—how is one to observe a bird of prey traveling nightly over a range of several miles?—our knowledge of owl anatomy has advanced rapidly. We know now most of the physical elements that constitute this efficient mechanism of death.

Only consider what equipment any nocturnal hunter ought to have to succeed. Enhanced senses would be useful, to locate and fix the quarry. A method of hunting that combined daunting power with swift surprise would be advantageous, in order not to waste time or energy in combat. Finally, good weaponry, honed cutlery, to ensure that, once a strike is made, the chance of escape or struggle is minimal.

Owls are among the very few predators that have evolved a prey-detection system involving the interplay of two senses, sight and hearing. The large eyes, fixed in their sockets, can see under conditions with up to a hundred times less light than humans require. Only begin with the fact that a Great

Horned Owl's eye is approximately the same size as a man's eye, though a man is three to four times as tall and thirty to forty times as heavy. Like humans', but unlike other birds', both the owl's eyes face forward at the front of the head, so the bird can focus them on a single subject, an aid in depth perception known as binocular vision. Then, like some birds', but unlike humans', the eyeballs aren't circular; they're tubular, or elongated. This allows the lens—cornea section, which gathers light, to be as large as possible relative to the rest of the eye. More light gets through. Another improvement on human vision is that the owl has a more versatile diaphragm, which can "stop down" like a camera lens to a speck in bright light or open extra wide in dimness to admit more light. The diaphragm muscles can operate independently of each other.

But this only begins to describe the specialization of the owl's eye. Let's go inside for further inspection. Within the retina of all animal eyes are the sensitive cells that respond to light by forming images. These are the rods and cones, named for their shapes. Cones are sensitive to the bright side of the light spectrum, seeing color for the most part. Rods are receptive mainly to low-intensity light waves, the kind that travel by night. The owl retina contains sufficient cones to see well, though colorblind, by daylight, but the rods are densely packed there in bundles far outnumbering the cones, giving the owl extra sensitivity to dim light. As if this abundance of rods weren't enough, each rod cell contains a little-known substance called "visual purple," which apparently reacts chemically with the smallest light wave and signals the brain, where an actual image is formed as a result.

Let's take it even further, into realms where science is only beginning to delve: eyeground color and eyeshine. The fundus oculi, or base, of the owl's eye is tinted yellow. Researchers are not certain what yellow-tinted fundi have to do with seeing at night. What they have determined is that in seminocturnal birds, where evolution out of true nocturnalism has weakened night vision, red tints are mixed with a smaller portion of yellow to make orange-colored fundi; but that, in true nocturnal birds like owls, where night vision is strongest, the fundi are always yellow. Finally, eyeshine is still another adaptation for improving vision in dim light. We notice eyeshine as that mysterious colored reflection bouncing back from a cat's or raccoon's eyes when a light is shined at night. A tapetum lucidum membrane behind the retina, acting as an accessory mirror, reflects light that has already passed through the entire optical apparatus once back again for a second pass through the light-sensitive rods. Cats obtain about 40 percent increased night vision from eyeshine. Owls haven't been measured but show evidence of intense eyeshine.

What a masterpiece of evolution, this owl's eye. What a miracle! Could Leonardo have invented better? Could Thomas Edison have tinkered up its equal? Practically every adaptation known in nature to improve seeing in the dark, the owl has. Practically every element of the eye has been improved. The owl cannot see in total darkness—no creature can do that, because total darkness is by definition the absence of all light, and vision ultimately depends on the presence of at least some light. But it can do everything but . . .

As for the owl's ears and hearing apparatus, they are, if anything, even more highly evolved. The owl's astounding auditory powers are probably second to none among living things. If you spent a cold, dark, sleeting January afternoon standing in front of the Great Horned Owl cage at the Bronx Zoo, as I did recently, you couldn't fail to notice that listening, for the owl, is hardly a passive activity. Take this grand old Great Horned perched on the barkless diorama stump the zoo has provided it, staring right through me as if I didn't exist. The bird's head rarely remains still for more than a few seconds. It dips, bobs, swivels, cranes forward, stretches up, twists down, retreats into the neck, rather like a radar scanner constantly repositioning. I hear nothing but the falling sleet. The owl is picking up sounds humans can't hear—too faint, or out of our frequency range. In fact, aside from the eyes, beak, and mouth, a sound scanner is exactly what the owl's face is—a large saucer designed to transmit and amplify sound waves to the ears and brain. The rounded facial disks, which give the grand old Great Horned its appealing, semihuman appearance, are actually composed of short, stiff layers of feathers. These feathers, controlled by the facial muscles, are oriented to oncoming sound waves. The facial disks are bordered by a narrow trough, where the sound waves are caught, concentrated, and funneled to the ears, hidden behind the disks (the owl's horns are actually false ears, having nothing to do with hearing). Like human ears, the owl's ear has a pre-aural flap, the operculum. But in an improvement over man, the bird can move the flap forward or backward like a cowl, orienting the ear to the sound source. Again, the actual and relative size of the ears is enormous. In a species like the Barn Owl, the outer ear reaches from the top of the cranium all the way down to the lower jaw. The eardrums within are equally great.

For more than a century, anatomists have noted that owl ears are neither symmetrically placed on the skull nor of the same size. The left ear is generally larger, lower, and opens downward, while the right ear is smaller, higher on the skull, and opens upward. They are also set relatively far apart, since the facial disks are so large. These asymmetries cause sound waves to arrive a fraction of a second later at one ear than the other. The sound will thus be slightly louder in the ear nearer the sound source, and the two ears will receive slightly different tonal messages. Using this information for comparison, the owl triangulates to form a precise impression of the sound's point of origin.

There is still another specialization to owl's hearing, a rare one in nature: owls hear higher-frequency sounds better than the lower-pitched sounds made by their own voices. Almost all other animals hear their own tonal range best. One need not be too clever to guess which animals most consistently produce the high-pitched sounds owl ears are especially sensitive to: mice, rats, shrews, voles, rabbits, and the whole host of squeakers the owl hunts. It seems likely that the owl developed this ability to hear rodents best solely to do in more squeakers. But what if the cunning mouse makes nary a peep? Observant naturalists have noted that dry spells in the weather are accompanied by a marked increase in the owl's nightly catch, as read in their pellets, while precipitation decreases hunting success. In very rainy weather, many owls apparently won't even attempt to hunt. When modern ornithologists took these observations into the lab, they analyzed sounds made by rodents scurrying through dry leaves. They found that important components of these rustling and crackling sounds are high-pitched in the very same frequency range owls hear most efficiently. Then they analyzed the sound of mice chewing. And chewing, too, it turned out, produces high-frequency sounds. Which helps explain why people have reported seeing owls suddenly plunge into perfectly undisturbed, deep snowdrifts and come back up with mice in their talons.

Just how precise these wondrous adaptations make the owl's hearing was the subject of a legendary series of experiments on Barn Owls by a then-Cornell ornithology student, now Dr. Roger Payne of Rockefeller University. As Lewis Wayne Walker described Payne's work in his *Book of Owls*:

> In his experiments Payne carefully sealed all the openings in a long shed so that the building was completely light-tight. Then dry leaves were spread on the floor and a Barn Owl given its freedom within until it had become accustomed to its dark surroundings. Time after time live mice were released and for just a moment Payne could hear the liberated rodent move in the dry leaves. Then he felt a draft of air as the owl left its perch and dived to the floor. When the light was snapped on, Payne found the owl with mouse in talons. He tried the experiment time after time with almost unvarying results. Owls were changed to make sure that the ability existed for the species, and was not just the ability of a single individual. Those from the west, those from the east, and some I sent him from Arizona all performed in a similar manner. Final confirmation that the owls executed their feats solely through the use of their acute hearing came when Payne commenced plugging the owl's ears. When this was done the owls went wide of their mark, baffled because they were deprived of the triangulation that sound gave to their aim. Unplugging the ears of one that had missed brought accuracy again, as well as the demise of another mouse.

Now let's take the final step into the owl's brain. Eric Kundsen, a California neurobiologist, recently put the Barn Owl, the same species Payne used in his experiments, on the cover of *Scientic American*. Kundsen took Payne's work one step further by attaching miniature electrodes to the owl's brain. Then he put the owl back in the blackened environment and started releasing rodents. The feedback he plotted showed that the owl's brain contains specialized neurons arranged in the form of a three-dimensional map of space. These brain cells process the messages forwarded by the asymmetrical ears into a precise mental readout on the horizontal and vertical distance of the sound source. The owl then lines up, so to speak, with its mental cross hairs and homes in.

The conclusion of these experiments is that owls can hunt perfectly well by hearing alone. This phenomenal auditory system seems to make the equally magnificent visual adaptations redundant. Owls are known to have two basic methods of hunting. They either perch above the ground, solemnly waiting for the telltale rustle, squeak, or chew to inform them that a meal is near; or, they patrol low over the fields, meadows, or scrub of the forest floor. It may well be that on dark, moonless nights the owl uses its keen eyesight mainly to avoid obstacles—tree branches, stumps, shrubs, rocks—while the ears, fixed on the prey, bring the bird in for the strike.

This hypothesis is supported by the highly economic adaptation of silent flight. Economic, because it serves a double function. In the first instance, the owl's silent flight keeps the prey unaware of its jeopardy until too late, adding the element of surprise to the owl's attack. In the second instance, no sound made by the owl itself will drown out the sounds emitted by the prey, allowing the owl to continue its auditory reading and to adjust its trajectory accordingly all the way to the target. Just as the predator's senses work in tandem, so, too, do the ears and wings coordinate.

Owls accomplish silent flight in two ways. One is that, under all their bulky plumage, owls have rather modest-size bodies. The Duke, for example, standing two feet tall with a gigantic four-foot wingspan, weighs about five pounds. Large wings relative to body weight mean that each square inch of wing has to buoy that much less weight aloft, which is called low wing loading. This renders the owl quite buoyant; buoyancy necessitates less wing flapping and permits more gliding. It's quieter to glide than to flap. The owl's feathers are also remarkably tailored to permit the passage of air without friction. Right now, I have two feathers before me, picked up off the ground in Pelham Bay Park. One is a nice, long, showy pheasant's plume that will soon grace my lady's hat. The other is the Duke's flight feather, found under the roost. Comparing the two under a hand magnifier, I see that the tips of the barbs on the pheasant's feather are stiff and thick. They will resist the air cutting through them like a flying frying pan, producing sound. The owl pinion, on the contrary, tapers to a soft fringe along its leading edge. Each individual barb ends in a downy, sawtoothed pile. These softened edges dampen the sound made by air rushing around them. They render the Duke and Duchess flying apparitions.

Having located its prey in the dark with these exceptional sensory systems, gliding down on hushed wings, the owl now brings into play its consummate weapons, the hooked beak and razor-sharp talons. Of these, little need be said, though much may be imagined. There are four talons on each foot. They are in zygodactyl arrangement, which means two facing forward and two back, like old-fashioned ice tongs. With a single launching flap, the owl sails head first toward its prey, talons tucked up underneath. At the last moment before striking, the owl goes into a quick reverse, thrusts its head back, and lowers the talons like landing gear. A branching tendon running between powerful leg muscles and bone claws operates like a sliding pulley, locking the talons into place as they rake into the prey. The claws are hard and sharp enough to pierce bone. They remain embedded until the leg straightens, releasing the tendon. By then, the owl's beak has already made short work, and the rodent's head is rolling down the owl's throat.

It's a real mismatch between the sneakiest, fastest mouse and the fattest, oldest owl. Maybe the owl has a bad night from time to time, or there's an occasional escape—a mouse with a Ph.D. in evasion, and three varsity letters in track and field. But never—never—has anyone heard of a mouse, rat, rabbit, or skunk subduing a Great Horned Owl. Nature can leave everything to chance, because she leaves nothing to chance.

# E L E V E N

There is another mythic tradition associated with owls, and that is the ancient Greek tradition of the owl as the bird of wisdom. Owls were the sacred emblem of Pallas Athene, the goddess of wisdom, and she was the owl's protectress. Sometimes she was portrayed with an owl emblem on the Corinthian helmet Hephaistos forged for her; sometimes she was called "the owl-eyed maiden." When the populist politician and apostle of Athene, Peisistratus, became autocrat of Athens in 556 B.C., he had new coins minted with the profile of Athene on one side and the owl on the other. How the owl became associated with Athene remains obscure. Some have suggested that Athene first emerged as a pre-Hellenic rock deity. The owl, at roost in dark crevices, became linked with her. It has also been thought that an owl may once have nested in a temple devoted to Athene. And then there's the theory that, early in Greek history, Athene became the local deity of Athens, and Athens must have had many owls hunting its open, hilly terrain. Over time, local goddess and local bird would have become intermingled in the Athenian mind. What these theories prove, mostly, is the poverty of the modern mind when it comes to transferring natural knowledge to the realm of the mythic imagination.

True, we know little concrete about the relationship between Pallas Athene and her blessed owls, but I've been dipping into the mythologists Bullfinch, Graves, and Steadman, and we certainly know enough about Athene herself to shed some light on the matter. The early Greeks were crazy for Athene. Even with their total awe of Zeus, their intense devotion to Ares and Aphrodite, the Greeks also knew the other major deities of Olympus as unruly, tempestuous, driven, and at times cruel. They permitted themselves only one goddess whose reputation was entirely unblemished, and they adored her as a doting father does his lovely daughter. Indeed, that's the meaning of *Pallas* in classical Greek: girl, virgin, maiden. The coins that portrayed Athene and her owl were known as *korai*, or "girls."

The Greeks took their girlish divinity from the earlier civilization of Minoan Crete, which was far advanced in the useful, beautiful, and domestic arts of pottery, jewelry, weaving, and especially architecture. From around 1900 B.C, the Minoan Cretans built elegant palaces, where royalty paid homage to a young "palace goddess." The Cretans worshiped nature, and their chief deity was the omnipotent Earth Mother. The Palace goddess represented her youthful, pre-maternal aspects: artistic skill, feminine intuition, and self-sufficiency.

These themes were already present when the early Greeks took over Pallas Athene and told the story of the goddess's birth. It seems that Zeus's wife Hera, without the help of her husband (or any male, for that matter), had given birth to a son, Hephaistos, god of the forge and divine craftsman. Zeus was so outraged, so furious, so threatened by the implication that his wife could bear children without him that he got a terrible headache. To gain relief, he summoned Hephaistos and ordered that his own skull be split open with a bronze ax. No sooner did Hephaistos's ax fall than the little girl with the wide, owlish eyes leaped from the gaping wound, dressed in a set of finely wrought armor. Thus Zeus's daughter emanated not from any womb but directly from the mind of God, the embodiment of divine wisdom.

But it was not wisdom as we understand that term today—the specialized Province of scholars and philosophers. The word *sophia* came to have that meaning only much later in Greek civilization. Originally, and up to about 400 B.C., Steadman tells us, *sophia* meant "adroitness of hand and brain: therefore, skill." It meant expertise, the ability to make and do things well. Athene was patroness of all skilled artisans, or, as Steadman says, "of every man and woman who is definitely keen and good at his or her job." In the same period, Athene was being portrayed in sculpture as a girl of about twelve. One of the best known figurines is in the collection of New York's Metropolitan Museum of Art. It shows the enchanting maiden dressed in a simple Doric chiton, holding her small owl in the raised palm of her right hand. So Athene is definitely identified with the owl in the period when *sophia* meant "knowingness." Could the early Greeks, or the Minoan Cretans, have observed the supreme skill and coordination that figure so prominently in the owl's existence, the prudence and craftsmanlike sobriety with which the owl goes about its work as a hunter?

As the girlish divinity, Pallas Athene remained aloof from the sexual intrigues on Mount Olympus. Not only was she the chaste virgin, but she remained so by choice, though gods, giants, Titans, and heroes all sought her love. In another myth, Athene asked Hephaistos to fashion her a new set of armor. Hephaistos became so enamored of the maiden that he readily believed the malicious prankster Poseidon when he said that Athene was on her way to the forge to pick up her armor, expecting to have violent love made to her, with her father's consent. Actually, Zeus thought a marriage between Hera's son and his daughter would stabilize the divine family, but as always he indulged his favorite child, giving Athene leave to reject the limping god's advances. When Athene entered the smithy, Hephaistos lunged crudely. But Athene was far too strong, and in the struggle that followed Hephaistos's seed spilled over Mother Earth, fertilizing her by accident. In due time, a boy child was born, but Mother Earth would take no responsibility for the misbegotten infant. Athene took the baby herself, named him Erichthonius, hid him in a basket guarded by serpents, and gave the basket to the daughters of Kekrops, the king of Athens, with strict instructions not to open it. However, the king's daughters disobeyed Athene by opening the sacred basket. When they saw the child with serpent's legs, they were so terrified they leaped from the Acropolis to their death. Athene took the baby back and raised him tenderly in her aegis. A strange and ambiguous legend, no doubt. But it does demonstrate Athene's unequivocal determination to stay true to her solitary nature. Athene's chastity is nowhere in mythology held up as a moral virtue, but rather as a reflection of her fierce independence. She does not reject motherhood in the myth—only the union with Hephaistos. This unshakable solitariness also happens to be a prime, if not *the* prime, personality trait of the owl. Most owl species are thought to be monogamous, at least for the duration of the nesting season. But even the monogamous owls are rarely seen in the company of their mates, and owls do not display any social hunting behavior.

If skill and solitariness were attributes Athene shared with her sacred bird, a third myth portrayed on the gables of the Parthenon binds them together in a still more profound way. In the story of Pallas Athene's bath, she once again appears as the maiden and girlish divinity. Athene's friend and inseparable companion was the nymph Chariklo, mother of the handsome young mortal Teiresias. One sunsoaked day the two females ventured afield together. It was hot and, coming beside a fair-flowing stream, they undid their robes and bathed. Only, Teiresias was ranging with his hounds nearby. By chance, he beheld the goddess naked. Though the indiscretion was involuntary, disaster was preordained, for viewing a female deity's body without her consent was strictly forbidden. When Actaeon viewed Artemis under similar circumstances, but with malice aforethought, she promptly set his own hounds on him, and they tore him to pieces. Interestingly, Athene punished Teiresias for seeing her by taking away his sight, that is, by blinding him. The poet Callimachus wrote, "She spoke and night seized the eyes of the youth and he stood speechless; for pain glued his knees together, and helplessness stayed his voice." Chariklo begged Athene to take back her words of anger and restore her son's vision. But Athene replied, "No sweet thing is it for Athene to snatch away the eyes of children. But the laws of Kronos order thus." In the end, however, Athene proved merciful. To compensate the youth and soften the harshness of his blindness, she granted Teiresias that deeper vision called inward sight and made him a seer, with the gift of foretelling the future. The very idea of a "seer" is sufficient reason to read this myth as not only a warning to steer clear of waters where immortals are splashing. It is more about seeing, and about two different kinds of vision, the one physical and superficial, the other intuitive, feminine, and prophetic. Athene, the owl-eyed maiden, controls the power of inner sight. Is it too much to suppose that the early Greeks associated Athene's visionary powers with the prominent eyes and extraordinary seeing ability of the owl, the bird that sees where humans find only darkness? My guess is that the Greeks—and the Minoan Cretans before them—knew a great deal about the owl, its physical characteristics and behavior. They were better observers of nature than we give them credit for: one advantage of worshiping nature is that the devout do fieldwork.

By the time of Phidias and Pericles, around 450 B.C., Athens was changing, and Pallas Athene changing with her. Phidias was the sculptor who put the legends of Athene on the Parthenon's stone façades, Pericles the politician who probably ordered the temple built in the first place—to the greater glory of the city-state. This explains much about what was going on. Athens under Pericles was emerging as an aggressive, militarist power, more in want of a glorified imperial deity than a young maiden, skillful, solitary, and visionary. From this time began the conscious transformation of the girlish goddess to emphasize her mature aspect as goddess of military strategy, spoiling for battle. Athene Promachus—"who fights in the front rank." Athene Alalcomeneis—"who repulses the enemy." Much later, Pallas Athene ended her days as the Roman Minerva, the brassy, broken-down goddess of war and commerce, hoisting a javelin or thunderbolt. Her sacred owl had long since flown away.

# T W E L V E

By most standards, the Great Horned Owl is a successful creature. To describe this nocturnal bird of prey requires mainly the superlative case. It is the largest and heaviest of all North American owl species. It is also far and away the most powerful of our owls. If you ever have the opportunity to actually hold a Great Horned Owl, you will come away comparing the strength of its talons to a locking vise grip, or perhaps a steel claw trap. It reputedly has the fiercest personality as well—not just of the owls but of all the North American birds of prey, including the falcons, hawks, and eagles. Eyewitness accounts tell of Great Horned Owls brazenly attacking bald eagles, driving away our national symbol of courage and might, appropriating the eagles' nests for themselves. Odor of skunk, fang of viper, claw of eagle, or army of crow, the Duke and Duchess go undaunted. The Great Horned Owl is seemingly not acquainted with fear.

While the Horned Owl can hunt, seize, and consume any of hundreds of species of rodents, lizards, amphibians, and birds, no predator hunts it. The Horned Owl has no natural enemies, and nothing can harm it, save man with his gun. As for distribution, another measure of a bird species' ability to survive, the Great Horned Owl is the most widely distributed of all North American owls. It is commonly found in all fifty American states and most of subarctic Canada. It lives in the scorching deserts of the Southwest and on the

snow-swept plains of the Midwest. It calls the dense forests
of Maine and Washington home. The steamy swamps of
Georgia and Florida prove no obstacle to the Great Horned's
residence. The frigid winter cannot drive the Great Horned
away—in fact, it takes the cold completely in stride, from
Montana to Alaska. Finally, and perhaps the harshest test of
all, the Great Horned Owl endures wherever man is, provided only it is not shot or poisoned. The Duke and Duchess abound on the farm, in the suburb, and they have found
the cities habitable—even our largest, most industrialized cities, where falcons and eagles have long since disappeared.
In sum, the Great Horned Owl appears to epitomize the
prototypical Darwinian struggle for survival. Dominant, surly,
unflinching, steely, individualistic, and marvelously well
adapted to its niche in the ecosystem, the Horned Owl is
truly the predator's predator. But the Duke of Pelham Bay
is not all mechanism and function. Even the mightiest of
owls has another side, too. Only, to know it, you must follow the owl deeper into the night.

It was four o'clock on a late January morning, moonless,
starless, and 15 degrees F. Black woods edged the blacktop
road under a sky black as any witch's sabbath as I started
down the road that led past Orchard Beach to Hunter's Island at the tip of Pelham Bay Park. You could not see the
breath in front of your face, and the darkness made you feel
alone and vulnerable, no matter how many times you'd been
out in it. In the parking lot at Orchard Beach, cars with their
headlights doused circled round and round. As I made my
way along the edge, a car flicked on its high beams. When
it rolled toward me, I ducked into the phragmites, wishing
I owned talons and swift wings. Had the human denizens of
night come to find the Great Horned Owl, too?

Beyond the road and into the woods, I headed toward the

dense stand of hemlock trees, took up my post, and waited. Within the hour, the sky softened to navy blue, and life began to stir. In the nearby bay, Canada geese beckled comfortingly. The flitting whistle overhead told me that canvasback ducks were already on the wing. Squirrels made their first morning chitters. Off in the underbrush, something crept oafishly home, crackling dry leaves underfoot. It would not be long now.

Then came the unmistakable bass hoots of the Great Horned Owl, returning from its nightly hunt. Immediately, all the other animals flew into panic. The squirrels raced up and down the hemlock branches so haphazardly that they tumbled and scampered to keep hold. Bluejays, suddenly alert, rose to the topmost branches and cawed an insistent alarm. That oafish something off in the underbrush fled for its hole.

And there was the Duke of Pelham Bay, perched in the barren branches of a hardwood tree, about a hundred yards off and just outside the hemlock grove. Through my fieldglasses I watched this magnificent creature, majestically plumed in demure browns, bays, buffs, grays, and whites, with huge yellow eyes the color of smoked meerschaum. The owl's attention was focused away from me, toward the deeper forest, where another Great Horned answered. The calls went back and forth in a willowy, low-pitched language:

"Hoo/hoo-hoo-hoo . . . hoo-hoo/hoo-hoo."

"Hoo/hoo-hoo-hoo . . . hoo-hoo/hoo-hoo."

Then casually, almost effortlessly, the owl glided in over my head with its tremendous wings fully spread, made a silent turn around the tree I stood beneath, and returned to its former perch on the border of the grove.

"I have duly taken note of your presence," the Duke was saying. "I am neither amused nor irritated. I am busy."

It grew marginally lighter. The owl flitted from tree to tree, describing an arc around the hemlocks, aligning itself each time to face the direction of the other owl's call. When he made his call, this Great Horned bowed as deeply as any Japanese ambassador and raised his white rump till the tail-feathers stuck straight up in the air. As the bird craned forward and hooted, he seemed to shake every last ounce of hoot from his puffed body. Then he waited for the return call with a concentration bordering on anxiety. The hoots coming back out of the forest from the female owl excited the male into partially lifting his wings, which I could now see were shivering. Then he repeated the entire performance. They hooted back and forth, the gap between calls shortening, until, at length, there was no mistaking it: they were singing a tender duet together.

Ah, Duke, you mighty hunter. Predator among predators. What is that strange sensation welling up in your aggressive blood? Could there be something more to this roguish life than carnage and feasting? How you tremble at the lady's song, you lovestruck Romeo.

The Great Horned Owl is the first bird in North America to court, mate, and nest, so this serenade was the true death knell of winter. Before St. Valentine's Day, the Duchess would be firmly ensconced on her nest, incubating eggs. The chicks would be born before the snow fully melted. And before the grass grew green once more, fluffy Great Horned owlets would be hopping from branch to branch in Pelham Bay, learning the fundamentals of survival in the big city from their proud parents:

*But let's not get too far ahead*
*Enough that winter's on the ebb*
*The rising sun dries chilly dews*

*The Duke's abroad with welcome news*
*Be tantalized with what's been seen*
*And satisfied with what's been said*
*Let's leave these lovers—*
*And home to bed.*

# SPRING

In the Parliament of Owls

# O    N    E

When W. H. Hudson returned from remote Patagonia to England at the beginning of this century, he found the ancient human dread of the owl's hoot alive and well. One dark and starless evening "tramping the Midlands," Hudson paused under a group of large elm trees, listening to the owls calling, when a local man happened across the ridgy fields. Noticing a form in the shadows, the man stopped short, then slowly inched backward. To allay his fears, Hudson quickly emerged, explaining that he had merely been listening to the owls.

"The owls—listening to the owls!" the man repeated in disbelief. But then, apparently deciding that no goblin would bother to supply such an explanation, he added, "We've been having too much of the owls over at Saintbury." He went on to tell the ornithologist that it wasn't a week since a young woman of his village, apparently in perfect health, had dropped dead after hearing an owl hoot during daylight in a horse-chestnut tree by her cottage. Now, a week later, the same owl was crying again, and no one knew who was marked for death this time. The whole village was in panic. The children had gathered under the horse chestnut to sling volleys of stones, but the stubborn owl had refused to come out.

Next morning, enticed by this "queer little story," Hudson set off on foot for Saintbury. The tale of the young woman's sudden demise was confirmed by a man engaged in repairing the thatch roof of a cottage near the very same horse-chestnut tree: the owl's hooting didn't bother him in the least. Owls, he coolly informed Hudson, often hoot in the daytime in autumn, and no one drops dead as a result. "This sceptical fellow," Hudson observed with satisfaction, "was a young man who had spent a good deal of his time away from the village."

But no matter how far we may travel from the village, a piece of the village travels with us. In every age the prejudices of previous ages lie dormant in our minds, ready to spring to life at the right opportunity. So much is clear when the nightbird's call penetrates our nerve paths wondrous strange, booming through creaky gates and cobwebbed chambers, winding back through forgotten tiers and cloisters and shadowed galleries, back past the Age of Enlightenment, past the Neolithic, until finally striking resonance in the dank caves of the Paleolithic. There we squat, in all our vulnerable nakedness, crowding the dying embers of our pitiful fires. Our nocturnal misery tell us that danger roams the gloomy night outside, and death sleeps with one eye open beneath the tree where the owl taunts. What form of beings lurk out there we can only imagine: no one ventures to find out. Those who try don't come back. So our religion is the celebration of chattering teeth and shivering bones, until some shrewd priest draws the owl's image on the wall, and claims control. We have reached the source of our owl fear.

The impressions that owl vocalizations have had on man, which cut across continents, across cultures, across time itself, cannot be forgotten. There is no possible way the identification of the owl's hoot with death and weird sorcery could have arisen in one place and spread to so many others. Owl images appear as early as fifteen hundred years ago in the ice-age caves of southern France. The earliest Norse legends suggest the owl was considered a bird of ill omen and it became a taboo even to speak the owl's name. Hudson's English countryfolk might conceivably have learned their owl fear from their Roman conquerors—but how, then, to explain the ancient Hindus' belief that to hear an owl near your abode foretold death, or that the Chinese peasant hears ghosts speaking through the owl?

Perhaps our own deeply intuitive and emotional reaction to the owl's call intimates that we share with other animals many levels of meaning in behavior beyond the instinctual and utilitarian. Owls convey an image of mystery to us—but why should the baying owl and its intended audience, other owls, feel less than we do hearing it? Indeed, the owl might feel more—the conflict of passions, the contradiction of instincts, the opposition of various adaptations. Every owl exercising its raucous dirge might well be expressing more than Descartes—or even Darwin—ever dreamed.

# T  W  O

It's probably not a bad thing for an owler in spring to wander over a variety of unfamiliar habitats. To learn something of the owl in spring it may become necessary to do what the owl does: lead the nomadic life and roam the countryside, hooting whenever appropriate.

So, on an afternoon in early May, I tossed my binoculars, sleeping bag, and tent into the car and set out to discover what I could of the owl's vocal habits. I'd arranged to begin my peregrinations in southern Connecticut, where Dr. Noble Proctor, professor of biology, would be leading his field ornithology class on a nocturnal expedition. When I pulled up to his house in the charming New England village of Branford, Dr. Proctor had just returned from an all-day Audubon Society conference. He was standing in shirtsleeves on his front lawn with his wife Carolyn, his younger son Eric cradled in one arm, his older son Adam running circles around his legs, saying good-bye to his in-laws who had dropped by, his mail and messages in his free hand while he discussed dinner arrangements with his wife. "Welcome," he greeted me. "If you like chaos, you've come to the right place."

Proctor is a burly man in his early forties, with a reputation as one of the best and most active professionals in the bird and botany business. An old-fashioned field naturalist, he is most enthusiastic when he can impart the tremendous body of knowledge he's accumulated to others. His life is crammed with teaching, conferences, lectures, writing, tours, and collecting expeditions. A well-scribbled calendar on the refrigerator door indicates the intensity and range of his activities. Already within the past month, he's delivered fifteen lectures on the birds and wild flowers of Connecticut, and on owls—a Proctor specialty. Five days hence he would be off to Alaska to lead a tour chasing pelagic birds. Then he'd return home for three days before taking off to Africa to guide another tour. Does all this frenetic activity run him down, burn him out? "Not a bit, I thrive on it," Proctor said. "What's exciting about my work is that every time I can show someone something they've never seen before, I get to see it as if for the first time."

The plan for the evening was dinner, then straight off to sleep. We would be rising at 2:00 A.M. and hitting a few owl haunts on our own before meeting his students at 3:30, then continuing our "owl prowl," as Proctor likes to call it, into the predawn. Afterward, the professor and his class would go on to a meadow to catch the woodcock's spectacular mating dance, then carry through the rest of the day after marsh birds, warblers, and shorebirds. The students could expect to see at least a hundred different species in the twelve-hour excursion, known in ornithological slang as a Big Day.

By 2:30, we were driving down dark country roads. The air was balmy, and the night sounds carried. We could hear a Barn Owl crying in the distance as it patrolled a local golf course. Dr. Proctor had been working this territory for thirty years, and the major change, he said, was the increase of cars and people out and about in the black hours. We passed all-night 7-Eleven stores, where kids stood zonked in front of video games. Coming around one curve, we passed a line of twenty cars going in the opposite direction. "It's really

incredible," said Dr. Proctor. "What are all these people doing awake at this hour? When we used to go for owls in the
sixties, the only vehicle we'd pass was a newspaper delivery
truck. When I look back over my old field cards, I see the
reference 'NDT' over and over again. That truck became
part of the nighttime ecology. You could always count on
getting forty-one Screech Owls and one newspaper delivery
truck. Humans have become much more nocturnal now.
We're free of the sunup-to-sundown rhythm of an agricultural
society. We're starting to live like owls."

We visited a few of the professor's tried and true Screech
Owl spots along the darkened roadside. At each one, Dr.
Proctor called into the trees. His Screech Owl imitation
seemed perfect, a long, descending, trilling whistle made by
gathering saliva at the back of the throat, then whistling
through it softly. The saliva imparts the trill or modulation.
Imitation owl calls, which owlers practice constantly, are designed to make the owl believe another owl has trespassed
its territory. They are especially effective in spring, when an
owl on territory is highly sensitive to both interloping males
and available females. We don't know for certain which sort
we are imitating, but probably an offending male owl, since
passing females would not initiate communication. When the
professor's calls failed to produce a response at first, he
switched to the owler's "squeak"—the imitation of the high-
pitched sound made by a hurt rabbit or other rodent.
Squeaking is done by loudly kissing the back of your hand
with closed lips. Dr. Proctor said he'd had some success with
this in calling in Great Horned Owls. You might wonder why
an injured animal would emit the very sound most likely to
attract the attention of its number-one enemy. It may just
be that the scream is a reflex reaction to pain, but it does
raise the question whether some form of communication

takes place between prey and predator. This does seem to
be the case in several other predator-prey relationships we
know of. In his book *Of Wolves and Men*, Barry Lopez tells
of an incident observed in the Canadian subarctic when a
pack of wolves approached two buffalo bulls and two buffalo
cows lying in the grass—three of them in good condition,
one cow lame. At each approach of the wolves, the three
healthy buffaloes paid no attention, while the lame cow grew
visibly more agitated. Finally, when one wolf came within
twenty-five feet, the lame cow stood alone and stared the
wolf right in the eye, as if participating in her selection as
prey. In a sense, Lopez suggested, the standing cow was
signaling, "I am the weak one, and my time has come. You
may take me that the other, healthy, ones of my kind may
live, that my species may survive." Lopez called this the
"conversation of death." Does the injured rabbit cry out, not
for aid, nor solely from pain, but from an instinct for self-
sacrifice, informing it that a quick, sure death in the owl's
talons is appropriate and perhaps preferable to pain and suffering?

It's possible, said Dr. Proctor. What's certain is that injured rabbits, mice, voles, and other small creatures do cry
out at times and that the cries do attract owls. Whether
instinct plays a role in the self-selection of prey is still highly
speculative. But nature hasn't given the owl the duty of crop-
ping small mammal populations as a means of testing the
nightbird's hunting prowess. Maintenance of the ecological
balance is as important to the survival of a healthy rodent
population as to the nourishment of owls. Perhaps the mouse
that squeaks at the wrong time is giving notice of its particular genetic weakness. Or perhaps the owl, sitting silently
on its branch monitoring the fields and forests, is particularly
attuned to the slightly odd, arrhythmic, out-of-sync move-

ments of injured prey. The slower, clumsier, noisier members of prey species may certainly be the ones less skilled at evasion and escape. In these ways, natural selection could also be making the owl's balancing work easier. Death, after all, is apparently something only humans fear. For the rest of the animal kingdom, death is simply a part of life.

After only a few minutes whistling toward one hilly woodlot, Dr. Proctor received an answer in kind, and a trim little gray Screech Owl came out of the woods and landed on a branch above our heads. Dr. Proctor shined his flashlight up. The owl sat for a minute, transfixed by the light, before deciding we posed no threat to his territory, and flying back to cover.

"I can usually count on getting Screech Owls here every spring," the professor said as we returned to the car. "It's perfect Screech Owl habitat: a small stand of hardwood trees beside open meadow, with water running on one side. They sit up in the trees, listening and watching the meadow."

"Why near water?" I wondered out loud.

"Possibly because Screech Owls fish," he said. "They are one of our most omnivorous owls. They've actually been observed waddling through shallow water to take fish, but whether they grip them with their talons, bottom fishing, or with their beaks, like wading birds, isn't known."

Dr. Proctor comments led me onto a trail of silent reflection. I was recalling how another Screech Owl I'd known twenty years ago had established itself on remarkably similar terrain—groves of low-lying, thin swamp maples, the fine, small meadows near at hand, the soothing stream close by. And how my childhood "hoot owl" had also established an uphill hooting perch outside my bedroom window. This situation, twice experienced, left an indelible mark on my consciousness. I could never again come upon those same conditions without immediately conjuring up the previous ones and deducing "Screech Owl." Each species of owl favors the particular habitat that it has been imprinted to recognize—not from the lessons of its parents but more likely from the conditions of its birthing grounds. Imprinting, in other words, must be a kind of emotional bond based in the memory and set off by the senses. It occurred to me that humans, too, are deeply imprinted in childhood. Later on in our mobile, wandering lives, we are never quite as comfortable, and perhaps never as emotionally stable, as when we replicate the conditions of childhood. Those born by the seaside seek to return to the seaside. Those raised in the mountains feel the ineluctable pull of heights. The force of imprinting seems to remain nearly as strong in us as in the so-called lower orders. For us, as for the owl, life becomes a journey back to its beginnings—if not to the actual nest site, then to a place that closely resembles it. A homecoming arouses deep emotions, and when an owl recognizes that it has reached familiar grounds, it is evidently stirred, and stimulated to cry out its anthem.

We met Noble Proctor's fifteen students standing in a dark, shivering knot in a dirt parking lot by a country crossroads, and together we walked uphill toward another of Proctor's trustworthy Screech Owl spots. The woodlot stood on a farm adjacent to fallow meadows, little more than two hundred yards from an old New England saltbox house. This time Dr. Proctor's whistle brought an almost instantaneous response. The gray Screecher came in to perch on a low branch above the group. It hung in for more than ten minutes, so placid and curious that each student had the chance to study the little creature in detail. The students were moved to "oohs" and "ahhs," as they might have reacted to a magic trick—and it was rather magical, the way Proctor whistled the owl up out of the depths of night, to perch nearby and be admired.

"Now, he's a male," Dr. Proctor lectured, "considerably smaller than the female. He's probably just eaten, which may account for his tranquility. Either he's got a nest nearby, or is heavily involved in nest-site selection. Probably, there's a female mate in a treehole nest nearby, sitting on eggs. That's why he isn't leaving. He wants to see what we'll do. We find Screech Owls in two colors that are called 'phases'—a gray phase and a red phase. The word *phase* is misleading, though. Screech Owls don't pass from one phase to another, as previously thought. The coloring may be related to the bird's habitat. We find a definite shift toward the red phase moving south in the bird's range, until, down in South Carolina, it's about 80 percent red phase. Around here in Connecticut, there's been a definite shift in the past ten or fifteen years, and red-phase Screech Owls have become a lot less common. Gray-phase Screech Owls have gone from around 60 percent of the total in the 1960s to around 80 percent at present. We don't want to keep a light on him for too long, so take a good look now. One time I was calling in a Screech Owl, and there must have been a Great Horned Owl waiting. As soon as I turned on the light—whomp! The Great Horned came in and carried the Screech Owl away. Let's get this guy back to his mate in one piece. Now if you'll follow me, we'll be heading for a low, swampy area to find Barred Owls."

We drove winding, hilly roads lined with stands of maple, white pine plantations, and neat, straight oaks. "We've had Barred Owls where we're going for six years running on the winter census," Dr. Proctor said from the wheel. "They are by far the most vocal of all the owls and they have the greatest range of sounds. There was one Barred Owl near here we used to hear, it would go on for hours, laughing like a maniac. 'Nyuk-nyuk-nyuk-nyuk-wow-wow-who-owwww!' It could do the most amazing things with its voice. We really don't know what the individual sounds mean. They're mainly territorial proclamations, but then you hear an extraordinary talker like that one and you think maybe this owl just *likes* to laugh. Barred Owls generally stay in one territory the year round, but there's some shifting that goes on in the winter when the swamp freezes and the food sources get scarce. It's not an actual migration; I'd call it more a 'spreading out.' A pair needs a larger winter territory to support themselves. I think that pairs pretty much stay together all year and that the male does most of the calling."

We left the cars on a soft dirt track leading into a narrow rift between heavily wooded hillocks, and Dr. Proctor reassembled his class. "We'll head back down the road, keeping the swamp on our right, trying to call the owl in," he explained in hushed tones. "Barred Owls don't usually respond right away. They like to think things over. So what we'll do is put out the call, then wait silently for ten or fifteen minutes to see if a bird responds. With Barred Owls, you never know. The male might fly in to check us out but sit silently high up in some branch watching us; we might never know he's there. The pair could also be sitting on eggs and not want to leave the nest, so the male might just sit tight and reply vocally. We'll have to be patient and silent and see what happens."

The Barred Owl, *Strix varia*, is a large owl, sixteen to nineteen inches tall, with a good-sized wingspan of about forty to forty-five inches, common in eastern North America. Both the Barred Owl and its western twin, the Spotted Owl, are easily recognized among the larger owls because they completely lack eartufts. The smooth, shapely head, large, brown, rueful eyes, and pale facial disks give the bird the rather mournful appearance of a shy person at a masked ball. This expression seems to suit the Barred Owl's demure personality and conservative demeanor. Though nearly as large as the Great Horned, the Barred Owl is not considered nearly so fierce—nor is it as reclusive as the western Spotted Owl. *Strix* is sometimes found making a meal of the smaller Screech and Saw-whet owls, but then the Barred Owl itself is prey to the Great Horned. It must be rather depressing to be a light-heavyweight contender in the forest food chain, only to bow before the more powerful heavyweights.

The Barred Owl's standard call is one of the owler's favorites, easier to reproduce by the human vocal chords than any of the others. It was one call of the Barred Owl's European cousin, the Tawny Owl, that Shakespeare immortalized in a ditty in *Love's Labor Lost*:

> *When blood is nipp'd and ways be foul,*
> *Then nightly sings the staring owl,*
> *Tu-who;*
> *Tu-whit*
> *Tu who—a merry note,*
> *While greasy Joan doth keel the pot.*

The Barred Owl's hoot is commonly set down nowadays as follows:

> *Who-cooks-for-youuu*
> *Who-cooks-for-you-allll!*

This transcription gives a fair approximation of the rhythm of a Barred Owl's call but fails to convey the right pronunciation and tone. In the first place, the first syllable is more

glottal than labial—not *wh* from the lips but *ch* from the back
of the throat. The overall timbre is a deep falsetto, and the
notes are B sharp, according to what a friend of Gilbert
White's found out when he tested them on a pitchpipe,
though modern pipers say the note is E. Barred Owls have
a habit of letting their final syllable slide downward, thus:
"Who-cooks-for-youuu." Also, the very last syllable of the
repeated phrase, transcribed as *allll*, actually sounds more
like *owww*—and should be barked or howled. Indeed, in
some localities, the Barred Owl is called the Barking Owl.

Dr. Proctor gave out his loud, throaty hoot half a dozen
times. When he finished, we stood stone still in the darkness
with our heads bowed, listening intently, as though the night
forest had become a cathedral. It was a full five minutes
before we heard a faint, timorous reply a long way off. As
we waited again in silence, this time trying to pierce the
moonless woods for the slightest movement, a second, even
fainter, hoot came to us from the direction of the cars. When
no owl appeared, we headed back up the road, and Proctor
hooted once more toward the black mass of conifers rising
above the dirt track.

"What we've got is two pairs," he whispered after a while.
"Probably pairs, because single birds would be more likely
to come in for a look. The road we're on seems to be at the
border of their respective territories. If we were to move
back up the road half a mile and turn into the woods, we'd
probably be right near the nest; and if we called from there,
the owl would more than likely come out to see what was
going on. But there's also a good chance that if we all
tromped into the woods together, we'd make so much noise
the birds would take off in distress. That's one of the limitations of working with a group this large, we can't always
work a territory fully."

"Aw, that's all right, Doc," one of the students piped. "We're all still amazed we saw the Screech Owl so fast."

"Well, of course, that was all arranged," Dr. Proctor replied deadpan. "I told him to be there at precisely three-thirty.

"It's amazing how fast it gets light this time of year," Dr. Proctor went on quickly. "If we don't get over to the meadow on the other side of these woods soon, we'll miss the wood-cocks. We'll be hearing them first, beeping from the ground before doing their aerial courtship dance. When they're up above dancing, you'll be able to hear the sound of their wings whipping back and forth. It'll sound like the high-frequency static on a shortwave radio. Then as the sky brightens, you'll be able to see them as silhouettes."

When we reached the gently rolling farmlands on the other side, the sky was blue-jeans blue, dressing for dawn. We followed the narrow lane that split the meadows in two. Close by, the woodcocks made their dotty beeps, but farther afield we heard the Barred Owls calling from where we'd left them, about half a mile distant. Three different owls now called from three different stations there, and they were really going at it:

"Who-who-whu-whooooo. Who-who-who-who-owwww!"

"Uh-oh-uh-oh-whu-who-who-who-owwwww!"

"Arrr-arrr-arrr-arrr-oooo-owwwww!"

They carried on as the dawn first broke, declaiming, disputing, laughing, snickering, yapping, barking, and howling at each other. It was a weird performance, but not hard to interpret. The end of the night signals the end of the owl's hunt, too, the hour when owls are on the move, looking for daytime roosts. Some might be exulting in the triumph of the kill, but most owls hooting in the wee hours are letting strays or interlopers know exactly whose territory they have wandered into. They are telling each other—and any Barred Owl that happens within earshot—to keep out, ending their broadcast night with wild territorial calls, each trying to outdo the other.

At length, with the light gaining, the songbirds could contain themselves no longer and broke into song. The owls shut down. And Dr. Proctor, standing on the brightening road surrounded by his keen students, was singing his own spring paean, accompanying himself with gyrating arms: "Over there, that's meadowlark," he crooned. "That 'drink your tea?'—rufous-sided towhee. Male cardinal in the trees. 'Beee-bzzzz': blue-winged warbler. Tree sparrow over there. Redwings sing, 'Konk-la-ru? O-ka-lay.' " He ripped off a dozen songs, to his students' utter amazement, then said, "If we use our ears and learn a few of the calls, we can appreciate much more than by relying solely on our eyes. Birds are vocal animals, and they communicate with their voices. When you learn to pick out one song from another, it vastly increases your knowledge of what's around you—and your appreciation of it, too. It's really great hearing all this stuff and knowing what it is."

# T H R E E

Having spent the winter absorbed in solitary hunting, the owl feels the spring urge and leaves seclusion to tell the world about it. From approximately the Ides of March, owls become progressively more vocal until finally, well established on territory, with doting mate on the perch and owlets in the nest, they become habitual hooters, swelling their throats to loose their less-than-musical ballads night after night, and sometimes hour after hour. When male owls first approach breeding season, their systems have not fully undergone the hormonal and physiological changes that will eventually double the size of their unsuspecting gonads. Before they have definitely laid claim to nesting grounds, established a hooting headquarters within their territory to hold forth from, chosen a nest site, or attracted a mate, cock owls are wont to wander from place to place, probing the night air with their voices to discover if there are already males established on territory in the vicinity. An established swain—already mating or perhaps in the process of courtship—sustains a great deal of positive reinforcement from *his* territory, *his* hooting station, *his* nest site, not to mention his moll. With this supportive environment stimulating the instinct for vocalization, the established male's vocal response to any stranger's challenge comes as a firm, loud, aggressive warning to the unattached one to steer clear. The pitch of various owls' notes is determined by the size of the air passage in the throat—the bigger the bird, the larger the air passage and the deeper the note, which is why small owls tend to whistle while the larger species hoot. Although the smaller owls are careful to disguise their voices through ventriloquism, all owls have control over their vocal volume. The excited territorial male projects his calls by assuming that special stance known as the booming posture—stretched up, puffed out, and straining. The obvious purpose of the booming posture is to throw the voice farther, louder.

Meanwhile, the unestablished, rambling male, whose biochemistry is not yet so keyed up, issues less assertive calls, weaker, uncertain. It is like the difference between questions and statements of unassailable fact:

"Hello there, anybody home?" queries the unestablished owl.

"*Scram!*" comes the territorial male's firm reply.

At this point, there are two options for the intruder: to get lost, as the established male has suggested, or to stand and fight. The determining factor seems to be timing. Time is of the essence for the itinerant male owl, for mating season does not last forever. If a cock owl has not located and established undisputed territory within the proper time frame, he's out of luck. He won't attain that full, self-confident quality to his call, and it's likely that only the culminated serenade alerts the female owl to the presence of a male fully capable and ready to mate. So the bachelor must move forward, impelled by the hormonal messages coursing through his bloating genitals. He has little time to waste challenging a territorial male. In this way, even as an owl emotionally proclaims his recognition of imprinted territory, vocal communication serves, in a second instance, to regulate fighting between males by largely reducing aggression to verbal challenge and retort. Such regulation also assures that in the end males will distribute themselves over the species' entire breeding range. Since males who would expend their energies in aggression would likely fatigue and perhaps injure themselves, and since crowding into insufficient territory would prejudice an owl pair's ability to feed their hungry, growing young, both outcomes of this vocal warning system are highly advantageous to successful reproduction. By conserving energy for the difficulties of parenting ahead, vocalization serves the survival of the species immensely.

Once the male owl establishes his territory, a major change begins to take place in his behavior. Contrary to what humans conjure up as the "natural" temperament of the sexes, the male owl now proves himself eagerly domesticated while the female remains something of a rogue, at least before committing herself to reproductive union. It is the male owl that inherits the disposition to secure territory, establish a homesite, put down roots, and await the love of his life—or the love of the year, in the case of the few non-monogamous species. The female owl inherits little of this homebody impulse. An unmated hen owl continues to roam freely from place to place to satisfy her instinct for a mate whose strong signals promise successful reproduction. While the male attends to the details of the courtship, getting a nest site ready for that moment when his bride-to-be comes wandering through the trees, the hen seems to have her mind made up from the start that she is mainly interested in one thing: procuring the very best opportunity for her offspring's survival. While the male turns hour by hour into the slave of raging hormones, the female owl initially acts the cool customer, the calculating one.

And well she must keep her distance and wits, for the mating of two powerful birds of prey is a difficult, delicate matter. Owls are built for destruction, not tender romance. Imagine a caress in the dark from those ganghook talons, or an amorous peck from that stiletto-sharp beak. A muffed show of affection could do a lot of damage. Potentially even more dangerous are the owl's highly developed predatory instincts. Should the hormonal and physiological transition from solitary hunter to docile mate remain incomplete, the female might fly to an expected paramour's side only to suffer a savage attack—or to launch one. Another factor is that male and female owls are generally undifferentiated by plumage. The potential exists for really disastrous crossed visual signals—a male mistaking a female for a rival male, for example, in which case the male's aggressive instincts might be unleashed, resulting in bloodshed.

Female owls are distinctly larger and heavier than their male counterparts. This is called sexual dimorphism, and it holds true not only for owls but for most hawks as well. Though a number of theories have been advanced to explain why female owls consistently outsize the males, one of the most convincing is that female birds of prey require a size and strength advantage to prevent their being mistaken for prey or rivals and attacked or killed during courtship and mating. A touch of intimidation may be an excellent way of keeping the male mind focused on romance, but the female owl is still wise to pursue potential mates with the utmost circumspection. She must have a finely tuned ear to recognize whether that hopped-up hooter over the next hill is going to make time with her—or try to maul her.

It's curious in this regard to compare the owl's spring mating call and its usual year-round territorial call with those of other birds, particularly the true songbirds, among which, I'm afraid, owls cannot be counted. Warblers, for example, make a variety of short, nonmusical chinks, clucks, binks, and gurks as territorial calls through the year, but when nesting season arrives these dowdy chirps blossom into fabulously flutey arias capable of melting the iciest heart. Of

course, it's outside the realm of natural science to make aesthetic judgments of birdsongs—and there's never been evidence that a talented tenor warbler makes a better mate than
an oaf who can't remember the lyrics or sings off-key. Yet
it's difficult to believe that the male warbler's liquid melodies
don't contain a component of pure and joyous languor with
which to seduce the female. Owls, by contrast, tend to do
little more in the spring than string together their usual year-
round territorial calls, repeating the same phrase over and
over again. In short, a kind of extended real-estate adver-
tisement. This is not to say that owls hoot without emotion,
nor that the call's effect on the female is one-dimensionally
utilitarian. Rather, it simply demonstrates that the territorial
and mating calls are less differentiated and developed in owls
than in the more melodic songsters. The close link between
these two forms of owl vocalization suggests that in nocturnal raptors one call evolved directly from the other. Probably
the territorial call developed first. Over time, the territorial
call evolved, as much as necessary, into sexual advertise-
ment as well.

No one can say with certainty the precise extent of the
territory owls require for nesting. The brothers Craighead,
who carried out extensive studies of raptor populations in
Superior Township, Michigan, in 1942, found Great Horned
Owls nesting in territories averaging 6.2 square miles per
pair, Screech Owls in territories averaging 2.9 square miles
per pair, and Long-eared and Barn Owls in territories of 37
square miles per pair (since the area they were studying was
37 square miles, the figures for the latter two species indicate that the Craigheads found only one pair of each nesting
there rather than the actual territorial needs of those species). When the Craigheads followed up the study in 1948,
they found Great Horneds nesting in 5.3 square miles,
Screech Owls in 2.5 square miles, and no nesting Long-

eareds or Barn Owls. The point is that nesting territories are variable and can under no circumstances be thought of in anthropomorphic terms—private property, owned by Mr. and Mrs. Owl, with nicely fixed borders like suburban house lots. Territories are fluid, particularly near the edges, and depend on the availability of prey species as well as on competition from other raptors.

The significance of territory, however, can hardly be over-estimated when you consider the voracious appetites of nest-ling owlets, who can eat their own weight in a day and grow to full size in eight to ten weeks. At the very least, owls must maintain territory during nesting season significantly more productive than the hunting territory necessary to maintain a solitary adult bird. If the young are to survive, the territory and its food sources must be ruthlessly guarded against competitors, particularly against those of the same species who would compete for identical prey items. This is why, despite the dangers involved, Screech Owls are more likely to be found nesting within a Great Horned's territory than close to the territory of another Screech Owl.

Since the owl cannot physically patrol its territory, major responsibility for guard duty falls to the bird's voice. It's less advantageous biologically that the owl sings prettily than that it hoots loud and clear. The deep, booming broadcast that humans often find hideous projects well, and is, all in all, a satisfactory horn for warding off other owls while attracting females. The male's spring mating call may not have the loveliest lilt in the forest, but it conveys the message to the female that a prospective mate has established and will de-fend territory, and is thus truly worthy of her consideration. Let the cock then present the hen with some choice food item, proving (1) that he can deliver the groceries and (2) that he's ready to make love, not war, and the female begins to ovulate, the only sign of love that counts in nature.

# F O U R

I headed north to hook up with my old mentor in birding, Michael Harwood, wild hawkman of Washington, Connecticut. Harwood was spending his free time in the Breeding Bird Atlas Project, the first attempt ever by conservation organizations to make a state-by-state census of breeding species. Over a five-year period, grassroots volunteer reporters will cover various territories across the entire country, compiling evidence about which birds nest there. These records can serve as an important data base for further research into all manner of questions relating to the flux of bird populations, but particularly into how development affects bird populations. Mike Harwood's territory in northwestern Connecticut encompassed rolling dairy pastures, hamlets and their budding suburbs, second-growth woods, pine plantations, and a large nature conservancy, as well as some virgin forest in the area's aged, peneplained hills. There was some potentially excellent Barred Owl nesting habitat there, so I signed on to help.

When I arrived, Harwood's spirits were aloft. He'd recently been working a heavily wooded section in one block of his turf along a steep river bank when a female goshawk suddenly burst from a towering pine, loosed a battle cry worthy of a kamikaze, dodged between the trees, and strafed Mike, nearly taking his head off. Harwood surmised from this that he'd discovered an active goshawk nest. The gos is thought by many to be the most beautiful of all birds of prey, with its banker's gray breast crosshatched by chocolate brown. An active goshawk nest would be a prize in any territory, and Harwood was bubbling with admiration for the courage Mama Gos had displayed in protecting her young by attempting to decapitate him.

Searching for owl nests is somewhat less risky than stumbling upon a nesting hawk. We devised a three-point program to carry out during daylight hours. Once we reached likely nesting grounds, or places where owls had been reported hooting (for many miles around, the inhabitants of the Connecticut countryside respond to the hoot of an owl by calling Michael Harwood), we would make imitation calls in the hope of convincing territorial sheriffs that a bad guy had arrived in town. If our bluff didn't work, we'd move to Phase II, covering the territory with a tree-to-tree search. Barred, Spotted, Screech, Saw-whet, and several other varieties of owls commonly use old woodpecker holes or natural tree cavities for nest sites; Barred Owls also use old stick nests of hawks and crows. An occupied nest hole will show signs of wear and tear around the edges, where the bird's claws have left marks as it went in and out. The traditional way of discovering whether such a nest hole is active is to thump the base of the tree with any handy rock or stick. If an owl is inside, she'll stick her face out of the hole to see what's going on—at least, that's the tradition: Harwood said he'd been thumping tree trunks for years without flushing a single owl. Finally, we agreed that if we were on promising territory, had thumped ourselves out, or had caught sight, as sometimes happens, of a promising-looking nest too high or too well hidden to peer into from the ground, then—and only then—would one of us climb the tree, to make a closer inspection.

Next morning we set off early behind a fast-rising sun. By

an hour after dawn, the dew had dried and the land lay warm as fresh biscuit, decorated by the winding stone walls, clapboard farmhouses, and handsome red barns of the New England countryside. For a long while we wandered the meadows and woodlots like tipsy fools, unable to resist all the singing, lovemaking, scrapping, nestbuilding, and incubating that make spring a carnival of life. Wherever we turned, nature's gay abundance greeted us with something new and delicious. In a field of Dublin green grass mottled by sunny yellow dandelions, male bobolinks thrust back their natty black and beige heads and faced off in ecstatic singing contests, abruptly ending in devilish chases whenever a female judge arrived. In a mud cliff behind a hardware store, bank swallows tore in and out of their nest holes with incredible agility, showing off their aerobatic tricks. Occasionally, they performed the act that tempts and defies the greatest human trapeze artist—mating in midair! Later, along the wooded edges of a high-tension power line, we thought we heard the marvelous stentorian gobbling of a wild turkey. Eager to see this American original, which has only recently returned from the brink of extinction to reassume its place as our pre-eminent fowl, we gave chase; but the swift-footed gobbler—if that's what it was—easily outran us. Then, in a pine plantation, a bomb seemed to explode right under our feet, and a female ruffed grouse cannonaded away on beating pinions. When we checked beside the fallen log she had emerged from, we found a shallow nest containing eleven beige eggs.

After noon we got down to the serious business of looking for owl nests. In the first spot we hit, a valley thickly covered with deciduous trees, our calls brought no response. But from a distant vantage point on the hillside sloping up from the notch, we could see a nest structure about two hundred feet off the ground, through a convenient parting in the trees. Our view was clear, but not in sufficiently close detail to see whether a bird was incubating eggs within. Yet the large stick-bundle nest had raptor written all over it. We made for the tree, but could not get into a position yielding a closer view. In fact, the nest was too well hidden in the leafy, lofty heights to see at all from closer up. After fighting our way though tangled undergrowth and scrub hemlock for nearly an hour, the only thing we managed to accomplish was to lose the tree to our view altogether, so we decided to move on.

The second site seemed more promising—a second-growth wood on abandoned farmland that contained a swampy pond. On the way down the road before turning into the woods, we met an elderly couple, who appeared to be on their way to a photo session for the L. L. Bean catalog, but were probably only out for a stroll. The man assured us we were on the right track, for the couple lived in a house nearby and often heard a notorious Barred Owl vocalizing in the woods. "Yuh," said the Yankee, "I can set my clock by that owl. Hoots at three P.M. sharp everyday—three P.M. on the dot."

"Odd time for an owl to hoot," observed Mike Harwood. "But Barred Owls can be eccentric bastards. Have you seen it?"

"Nayuh," said the Yankee. "Seems to stay pretty well back in the woods by the pond, theah. Now why is it that an owl's attracted to water like that? Don't fish, do they?"

"Yes. Sometimes. And they do seem to favor swampy habitat," said Harwood. "It may very well be that this owl's chosen a hooting perch near still water so its voice will project better. Well, we'll be off. Thanks much."

"Good luck," said the couple.

We entered the woods and soon reached the pond, over which hung many dead, knobby limbs suitable for an owl hooting station. Seeing nothing, Harwood gave out his best Barred Owl call, a bloodcurdling, chortling thing ending in a wild, throaty bark that could stir the dead.

"Well, that ought to do it," I complimented my companion.

We stood freeze-framed, facing opposite directions like a pair of china bookends, until a softer, willowy hoot came in answer, seemingly from deeper into the woods, though you can never tell. We tried to follow the voice, scanning each likely looking tree for a few hundred yards into the conifers. But here the ground was dry, and the twigs and needles snapped and crackled beneath our feet: there's nothing more annoying than the sounds of your own clumsy feet stomping and crunching sticks when you're trying to sneak up on an owl that has supersensitive hearing. To make matters worse, a local dog rambling through the woods decided we'd come for the express purpose of playing with him and bounded about us, barking happily. After a while it seemed certain that the owl had observed us and made for deeper cover.

Past midafternoon now. We had been so preoccupied we had completely failed to notice that cloud cover had moved in. The spring air, sweetly scented with violet and columbine, marsh marigold, campion, and fumitory, was now swept by the forceful smell of ozone. Mike had saved the best spot for last, a heavily forested mountain ridge rising over Lake Waramaug and known as the Pinnacle. Local birders had been counting Barred Owls on the annual bird census here for several years in a row. We drove the camper past the miniature resort cottages by the lake and up the old logging road as far as we could, then continued uphill on foot. The road rose rapidly. Huffing and puffing, we ascended, until

we reached a fork where a narrower footpath branched off
the road. Here we started to call, just as a light sprinkling
rain began, not at all bothersome. When there was no reply,
we moved ahead on the logging road, but soon left it to
scramble up a large shale outcrop.

"Hello," Harwood called from a short distance. "This looks
interesting."

At the top of the boulders, he was standing over the feathered remains of several common flickers, a bluejay, and as-
sorted other avian victims. The trail of down and fluff twisted
twenty feet back through the bushes, looking as though
someone had wantonly murdered a pillow.

"Bless my soul, a feeding station," said Harwood, referring
to the habit shared by many hawks and some owls of re-
moving their freshly caught prey to a private place in the
forest, quickly consuming the head as an appetizer, then
calmly plucking out the feathers before downing the main
course. The discovery encouraged us to repeat our calls, and
this time a pair of Barred Owls got going in response. It
sounded as if one was directly below us in the direction of
the lake and the other on the far side of the ride to our east.
Given the time of year, and the high probability that the
feeding station—if it was theirs—was well within nesting territory, we knew we were getting warm. Probably, one of the
pair was calling from the nest, or very close to it, so we split
up to look for both owls, Harwood descending, while I took
the high road.

In a few minutes' climb I reached a small swamp in a
hemlock thicket, which looked quite promising. I could sense
strigidian presence, and there was nothing mystical about it:
when you go into the woods for owls, you reach a state of
mental clarity in which your senses, your logic, and your
memory all start to work together; this liberates your native

intuition, and quite suddenly you're operating on a higher plane of knowledge that is more familiar as our so-called sixth sense. I scanned the trees quickly but, not wanting to give my position away to the owl any more than necessary, retreated back downhill to fetch Mike.

Harwood, meanwhile, had entered a stand of truly mammoth pines—perfect owl nesting territory—and was even more convinced than I that he'd found the right place. To test this notion, I let off a good hoot. The call was summarily and angrily returned from up the mountainside, but not from the conifer stand nearby. We agreed it likely that we were now indeed close to the nest and that the hen owl was keeping silent and sitting tight. This called for close visual investigation, which is time-consuming. You must get positioned exactly right to inspect the upper heights of each tree, most of which disappear above the base into a dark thicket of massed needles, or are hidden from every conceivable angle by their neighbor trees, or contain masses of sticks and leaves that look like nests but that you can't see into from below. Thus for several long and frustrating hours our eyes were glued to the binocular eyepieces, while whispers shot back and forth:

"Little to the left."

"No, to the right more."

"Got it now?"

"There's a goddamn branch in the way."

"Forget it, it's a squirrel's nest anyway."

For a change, we moved to the swampy uphill spot I'd reconnoitered earlier and repeated the whole process. When we called from uphill, one of the owls responded from down below. But when we hooted from below, the owl hooted back from above. Although sometimes, it's true, they called from someplace entirely different, perversely ventriloquizing. They were having excellent sport with us. And they had every right to—after all, it was their territory, not ours. At length, we'd been uphill, downhill, and aroundhill so many times we were beginning to resemble pack mules. We'd narrowed down our choice of probable nest sites to several likely looking trees. The owls were up there, they had to be, but we just couldn't get a bead on them with our fieldglasses. I threw myself down on the soft pine needles and rolled around in despair, crying, "I'm done in. They've beaten us."

"Beaten us? Why, we've hardly started," replied the game Mr. Harwood. "Time to get your climbing spikes on, boy."

"What climbing spikes? I don't have any climbing spikes."

"Pity," said Harwood. "It'd be so much easier for you with climbing spikes. But remember, you volunteered to climb."

"I did?"

I gritted my teeth, girded my loins—and tied my bootlaces. My previous career as a tree climber had ended at age twelve, when I climbed one to smoke a cigarette, fell out of the crown, and landed with both forearm bones protruding through at the elbows. Nevertheless, I handed Harwood my guide book, fieldglasses, and rucksack, and told him to notify my family if I failed to return in solid form. Then I saluted my opponent, a stout Eastern pine, and started up. Luckily, the tree was heavily branched right up to the top. Except for some minor slipperiness, the climb proved a breeze—though I moved up it more like a three-toed sloth than a chimpanzee.

What I hadn't counted on was the tremendous size of the stick nest overhead. The closer I got, the farther its edge seemed to cantilever out. When my head was directly below, the tight mass of sticks and leaves formed a ledge two feet wide. I would have to get a firm hand- and foothold, then bend over backward and crane out and up to peer over the top. My scalp, rising out of thin air, would be the first thing a female owl sitting in the nest would see, and it was my considered opinion that she would not take this in good humor. Holding tight, I performed my contortion, stretched on tiptoes, and peered cautiously over the edge. It was a nest, all right, but an abandoned one. Instead of a Barred Owl, there were only the remains of a Barred Owl's supper.

"Well?" shouted Harwood from below.

"Another feeding station," I called down. "Downy white feathers. Looks fresh."

"If they've got young, they might be plucking prey close to the nest before feeding time," said Harwood.

I retreated down the pine trunk. We continued to try to get position on the nests and cavities in the trees for a while longer, but the heart was going out of our search and, as the light rain kept falling, we grew not only frustrated but wet and miserable to boot. During all this time, a pair of Barred Owls—and possibly, their newborn offspring—were probably less than a hundred yards away. How much more often do owls observe men than men observe owls.

Don't imagine that humans are the only ones who have trouble seeing owls in front of their faces. Owls have problems identifying other owls, and this might make for big problems during courtship and mating if they could not locate each other by voice. Male birds on the whole possess two means of getting themselves recognized by females as potential mates. The first is to occupy a position where they can be readily seen and then display their attractive breeding plumage. The other is to produce some kind of mating song, audible and identifiable to the female, that she can follow to the assignation. Most birds combine visual and aural signals, but owls, as nocturnal creatures, largely lack the first option. The same adaptations that have made owls so well suited to the nightlife greatly reduce the chances of prospective mates recognizing each other by sight. Of course, no species could stake its survival on the slim hope of a visual encounter in the darkness and maintain itself for long.

In fact, much owl courtship activity takes place in the crepuscular hours at dawn and dusk. But owls are maddeningly difficult to detect even in full daylight. To see why this is so, only imagine a new variety of owl—the Dandy Owl, it might be called. The Dandy Owl has brilliant iridescent green plumage, lovely rose-hued breastplate, flashing golden wing coverts, and long tail plumes of magnificent carmine (once highly prized for ladies' millinery). A real looker, our Dandy Owl: very beautiful, very impractical. The Dandy

Owl has a life expectancy numbered in days. Not only does every predator in creation, including hunting humans, sneak up to attack it at roost, where it sticks out so brilliantly from its surroundings; but the small mobsters line up by the thousands to have at it, and soon harry the Dandy Owl to utter, sleepless exhaustion.

Real owls have adopted defensive strategies against such threats. The owl's demure livery camouflages the bird during enforced periods of daytime rest, when the owl is most vulnerable. Protective coloration, as it's called, can take numerous and subtle forms, but owls employ the three most fundamental principles of natural camouflage. First is color resemblance, the general agreement between the bird and its background that allows it to blend in. Just as the majority of animal life in the desert is buff or yellowish in color, and the fauna of the jungle fundamentally greenish, the owl of the woods is the color of tree bark, the Snowy Owl of the Arctic flecked white. Second is countershading, or obliterative shading, according to which an animal's coloring is darkest where it receives the most light and lightest where it receives the least. This has the effect of eliminating relief and rendering the creature optically flat. Vision depends in such large measure on the recognition of shape, informed by shading, that through countershading the owl appears as empty space, through which the background is seen. The barrings, crosshatchings, and complicated patterns of the owl's feathers are beautifully suggestive of a forest vista seen through twigs and tree trunks, while the white breast reproduces sky vista. Such deceptions of pattern and color are known as disruptive coloration, because they lead the eye away from the owl's form. To complete the illusion, owls adopt characteristic and instinctive "cryptic postures." Long before you are near, for example, the Long-eared Owl has heard your approach, narrowed its bright eyes to mere slits, compressed its feathers to half their normal width, elongated its body to twice its normal length, and thrust up its ear tufts. The bird actually assumes the shape of a stick or stump. Moreover, the more tightly a bird's feathers are pressed against its body, the clearer its markings become, so the posture itself is an essential adjunct of the obliterative equipment. In this way, owls fulfill the childhood fantasy that when you close your eyes, you disappear.

But owls have solved the problem of keeping concealed during daylight hours at a high price: they no longer have available the advantage of recognizing mates by plumage display. Practically the entire burden must be borne by the voice—at least until compatibility has been firmly established, and the pair comes together to preen and coo.

So many problems in reproduction: no wonder the Barred Owl, the Great Horned, and the Screech Owl, too, have developed monogamous habits and remain on the same territory year round. There is always a dialectical tension in nature, with the interests of the individual animal for survival set against the needs of the species as a whole. The owl's hoot is part of the creative synthesis of this conflict: in the end, an animal will adopt whatever measures are necessary to ensure that its genes will be passed on to future generations.

The Pinnacle above Lake Waramaug seemed such a good owl listening post that I decided to establish my own territory. I rented a small house nearby, determined to spend the month of June doing nothing but listening to the Barred Owls: an owler's holiday. The mountain, which was no more than a thousand feet high, had a number of things to recommend it as an informal study area. For one, it was well away from any large town, with its noise and artificial lights, yet provided with easy access on foot up an old logging road. It was also remote enough that I would almost be sure no other humans would intrude. But the main thing was that Barred Owls had firmly settled the territory, and so the site would likely offer opportunities for learning something about the role of vocalization in mating and nesting behavior.

Four or five times a week, I'd hike up into the woods simply to sit on a rock and listen. Sometimes I used the old logging road, which followed the contour of the mountain, and sometimes I headed straight uphill on the narrow footpath. I was certain by this time that the owls had their nest in the ridgy pine forest between these two paths and were using the cuts as flyways in and out of the nesting grounds. With plenty of time to search each tree, finding the actual nest hole presented no problem, but then the weather intervened in the form of torrential rains. I dearly wanted to see the nestlings—particularly to hear what parent and child had to say to each other—but after a struggle with my conscience, I decided not to disturb the owls by getting too close to their nest.

They were having enough problems. The tiny spritz of rain falling the afternoon we first visited the Pinnacle in late May turned out to be the front line of a wet weather system that didn't quit for the first two weeks of June. The month began with driving downpours, overflowing rivers, flooded towns, washed-out roads, ruined crops, a dozen human fatalities, millions in damages, the governor on the radio. It was undoubtedly even more desperate for owls in the midst of raising nestlings. A soggy forest floor provides soundproofing for rodent prey, making hunting extremely difficult just at the time when it's most crucial to the survival of the young. In addition, the heavy, rolling fogs accompanying such fronts throw owls off course, or shroud them when they raid foreign territories. The difficulties of maintaining territory are exacerbated. I could almost believe I heard the Barred Owls' sense of growing exhaustion in their daily predawn territorial declamations. Both partners participated in this heavy vocal labor, sending out a savage and terrible din. Instead of the usual "Who cooks for you?" both male and female were adding a syllable, as follows: "Who-cooks-cooks-for-you!!!"

After ten continuous days of rain, the forest was one great, sopping sponge, the trees a mass of undifferentiated green-black. The rain and continuous fog robbed the underlying flora of all individuality, with the single exception of the mountain laurel, which somehow blossomed pale pink clusters of flowers, each one with a pert cherry-colored star circling the stamen. But except for this sturdy splash of color, the early summer woods were a hopeless blob. The logging road turned to rivulet, and the rivulet to gaping mudhole. I put on waders and continued my increasingly morose excursions. For now at night the owlets made their hunger calls into the cold, drenching rain. They sounded like a whole group of matrons in an English murder mystery, all being strangled on the moor at once. Fog and lightning, lightning and fog. But only once during these nights of starvation were the owlets' pitiful cries answered, far off, by a "food is on the way" call from one of the parents—a distant series of short, subdued barks in rapid succession, more a rumor than a reassurance: "Ooh-ooh-ooh-ooh."

By the time the rains began to let up, the hunger calls had died; and when the sun finally peeked through, it was evident that the nesting was a failure. In the clearing morning, the owls' territorial calls had a distinctly melancholy tone. The proud duets of the mates stopped—only one owl hooted now. A few days later, the territorial calls ended altogether. When the owls failed to respond to my calls, I had to conclude they'd moved off territory—disconsolate or, more likely, recuperating from their hapless labors.

The next time I saw the male *Strix*, a week later, he was more than a mile away from the nesting grounds, in the hay fields surrounding the rear base of the Pinnacle. It was already past eight in the morning, and the owl had a wrathful band of bluejays and songbirds in hot pursuit. He gave them a contemptuous flap of his heavy wings, accelerated, and easily left them behind as he hit the edge of the woods. Perhaps he'd been caught out hunting late, trying to rebuild his strength for a second attempt at nesting. Barred Owls will commonly renest if their first attempt fails and there's still time to raise young before cold weather sets in.

Then something extraordinary took place. The end of my month at the Pinnacle happened to coincide with a rare total lunar eclipse. I took a last run up the mountain to watch the moon blush, shine crimson, and then turn into the very masque of the red death. It was half-past two in the morning when I reached the granite summit of the mountain. Row upon row of silky hills stretched before me in a voluptuous, feverish glow. Suddenly, the Barred Owls on the Pinnacle came alive, and they weren't alone. Off to the south, another hooter had picked up their rhythm. Farther north, still another. And then, as though the moon were conducting, the owls' voices rose over the peaceful countryside like a great, tempestuous chorus. You could hear the excitement in their voices. The eclipse was driving them to howling paroxysms, but they never sang out of turn. Even at their most raucous and horrific—for this was a midnight mass sung by completely unmusical prodigies—they seemed never to lose a certain order. They went each in turn, south to north, like a long, dyspeptic relay. They hooted in waves until the moon sank.

I became convinced through these episodes that someday an attentive, sensitive, and patient naturalist would actually construct a dictionary of owl communications. What will be remarkable about his lexicon is not that the hooting of owls will be found to have meaning but that each hoot will have two, three, and even more meanings. With only a narrow range of sounds available to them, already strictly determined in pattern and timbre, owls can convey information, subtle and complex messages, as well as emotion. Imagine our own powers of speech and communication reduced to such a sad lot, and marvel at what owls have accomplished by husbanding a threadbare vocal talent—turning those accursed hoots to immense biological advantage. In vocalization, as in much else, the owl adapts.

# SUMMER

## The Decline
## and Disappearance of the
## Short-eared Owl

# O N E

On May 14, 1921, Charles Anderson Urner was out birding in the salt marsh near his home in Elizabeth, New Jersey. He'd been working this section of the Jersey Meadowlands most of his life, but Charlie Urner was a crack birdman, president of the New York Linnaean Society, and not one to let down his guard on his own home turf. Thus when he came to the edge of a scald in the salt hay and flushed a Short-eared Owl, Urner knew he was onto something interesting. The bird leaped fifty feet into the air but, instead of flying away, it suddenly began to struggle. It fluttered, the wings went rigid, and the owl tumbled down through the air with a piercing cry, collapsing onto the ground a few feet away from Urner in the tall grasses. Then with one wing tucked under and the other flapping like a flag—and facing him head on—the owl dragged itself clumsily across the brush, all the while groaning, hissing, and barking in deep distress. When the bird thrashed into the air again, it was only to rise a few feet, shudder, and fall once more. To an untrained eye, the owl gave every appearance of being critically injured. To Charlie Urner, the owl was performing that splendid melodrama known as "the wounded-bird ruse," as if to say, "Hey, look at me. I'm shot. I'm crippled. I'm done for." Charlie Urner knew the purpose: to divert his attention from the Short-eared Owl's nest close by.

Urner walked on, ten yards into the bare spot among the *Spartina patens*. There a second owl flushed, joining its mate in the wounded-bird ruse. A third owl, apparently alerted by the alarm calls of the first two, rose in the distance, gained sufficient altitude to see what was going on, but did not approach any closer. When the feigned-injury act proved useless, the owl mates came to in the wind, glided over Urner's head, and hovered there together in silent vigil.

Urner had marked closely the spot where the second owl flushed. Proceeding there, he found the owl nest. Later that year, when his field notes of the occasion appeared in *The Auk*, Charlie Urner would conclude, with characteristically understated pride, "So far as I have been able to determine, this is the first nesting of Short-eared Owls definitely recorded for northern New Jersey."

The rudimentary nest on the meadow scald was composed of only a handful of matted hay, haphazardly drawn together from the immediate surroundings, but sufficient proof that, practically alone among larger owls, Short-eareds indulge in some nest-building activity (the Great Horned simply chooses the nest it wants and evicts the current tenants; Barn Owls have been known to lay their eggs on bare concrete). Inside the nest, Urner found eight tiny owlets, downy dumplings with huge heads. Perhaps he remembered the old English proverb, "The owl thinks all her young ones beauties." In any case, the young were of considerably different sizes. On one side squatted four larger nestlings, with their eyes wide open. Urner measured them and found they were five inches in length. He picked them up, drew their miniature wings apart, and inspected their light, cream-colored plumage, finding that their primary flight feathers had already developed to about an inch in length. The four smaller nestlings, cozied together at the other side of the nest, still had their eyes shut. They were only three inches long, and showed only the grayish fluff of newborns.

Urner returned one week later, on May 21. This time, there were only four owlets in residence. They had opened their eyes, and measured five and one half inches long. Urner surmised that these were the four smaller newborns he'd seen a week ago; the larger quartet had apparently already left the nest. They were probably hiding in the nearby grasses, flattening themselves against the ground as defenseless young ground birds do instinctively to escape detection. Again Urner was treated to the wounded-bird ruse by the parents. And once more, the vaguely mysterious third owl appeared, still maintaining its distance. On his third visit to the nest site on May 28, the nest was empty except for one dead owlet. Only one adult bird strained and shrieked overhead in simulation of injury, probably indicating that the surviving young were still close by, hiding from the intruder.

Charlie Urner went home to reflect on his discoveries. What intrigued him was how different in size and development were the two groups of four in the same nest, as well as the way that third Short-eared had lurked in the vicinity, taking more than a casual interest in the goings-on at the nest site. Urner knew that Short-eared Owls are reputedly monogamous. He also knew that one of the signal adaptations of the owl family is synchronous hatching. The clutch of owl eggs, laid over a period of days, develop at slightly different rates so the whole brood hatches more or less at the same time, nature's way of giving all owlets an equal opportunity to wrest food—and thus survival—from their parents. Yet these young Short-eareds had obviously hatched about a week apart. Urner thought it likely that the two groups of four represented different broods. But if so, how had they come to be in the same nest? Urner checked his weather records. On May 4 and 5 of that year, a heavy spring storm had struck the Meadowlands; an unusually high tide had inundated the greater part of the marsh. The scald where he'd found the nest was one of the few spots left unflooded. Was it possible, Urner wondered, that one or both broods, as eggs or young, had been carried by their parents from the flooded tidal marsh to this safe haven? Urner had never heard of owls moving their young, and so was careful to add in his journal article, "This is, of course, mere conjecture." The distant presence of the third adult owl, at least, distinguished conjecture from wild speculation. Urner decided to pursue the matter further at the first opportunity.

The following year, on May 22, 1922, another Short-eared Owl nest was discovered by a local farmer's boy cutting the salt hay on the Elizabeth marsh. Incubating Short-eareds are notorious for sitting their eggs closely, not flushing until actually touched. And that is just what happened. The boy couldn't see the nest, hidden in the thick tufts of *Spartina*. His scythe came down, striking the mother owl across the legs, and breaking one of the six white eggs she was incubating. Charlie Urner was called that night. By the time he arrived at the nest site next morning, however, the five remaining eggs had vanished; the adult owls were nowhere to be found.

On June 24, Urner returned to the scene of the accident, in the hope of finding some new evidence. Making his way through the grasses, he flushed an adult male Short-eared Owl, which immediately went into its injury routine, showing alarm by its rasps and repeated dives. Urner began to beat the bushes for its mate, but only after a careful, clump-by-clump search did he start her. To the ornithologist's satisfaction, she was apparently the same bird the farmer's boy had injured—alive and well enough, though she had trouble landing; when Urner later watched her hunt, he noticed that the accident had left her talons inutile. She was diving for prey exclusively with her bill, headlong into the reeds. Regretfully, Urner wrote in *The Auk* of January 1923, "I was unable to locate the young, though the constant anxiety of the adults made me certain of their presence."

It was not until a third tramp through the marsh, on July 1, that Urner finally located three young Short-eared Owls. Two of them were already fully feathered and able to fly, which they did as soon as Urner flushed them. The third was only barely capable of clearing the grasses, making fifty-yard hops before setting back down again. By now, Urner was excited by the probable correlation between the five eggs that had disappeared after the accident on May 22 and the three young owls associated with the injured hen. Urner saw the strong possibility that the uninjured parent had carried the unbroken eggs 150 to 200 yards from the old nest to the place where he'd flushed the family. For the second time in two years he had prima facie evidence that Short-eared Owls move their endangered young, though he had to admit there was "the chance that the young were from another brood, and that the association was accidental." What Urner required was a second form of corroboration that the three fledglings had actually hatched from the disappeared eggs.

On July 4 of that year, Charlie celebrated Independence Day by birding a different section of the Meadowlands, far from the first nest site. Walking these well-drained lowlands, Urner came upon yet another adult Short-eared, which by its frantic feints and barks hinted at the presence of a second nest site. Urner continued, "Careful hunting finally brought forth its reward. The mate rose, almost from under my feet, from a clump of goldenrod, a thick growth about two and a half feet high. In the shaded center of this clump was the nest, containing one egg and two young." Since the young were about five inches long, downy-coated, but with primary feathers developed to about half an inch, Urner decided they were at about the same point of development as the brood he'd found the previous summer; he judged them to be nine to thirteen days old. Returning to this second nest site on July 23, Urner found the unhatched egg still in the deserted nest—a dud—and one of the young owls, now almost fully feathered and nearly full-size, about seventy-five feet from the nest. When Urner approached the young owl, it beat its wings valiantly but couldn't quite lift off. When he bent down to pick it up, the owlet snapped its mandible angrily, flipped over on its back, and flailed away at him with its sharp little talons. Urner was reminded of the way marsh hawks defend themselves, made a note of it, and went away.

On his third and final visit to the site on August 2, Urner saw both parents perform a less urgent version of the wounded-bird ruse. He also flushed the young owl again. It could not fly well, but Urner assumed that "evidences of parental concern in birds continue only so long as the young are dependent upon the adults for food." If so, the hatchling he'd discovered at nine days old back on July 4 was still not completely independent at age thirty-eight days on August 2. Urner estimated from these admittedly "incomplete observations" that the period from hatching to fledging in the Short-eared Owl is somewhat over one month. Then he went back to the data on the nest where the accident had taken place. From the time the eggs disappeared on May 22 to the day he'd found the young owls fully grown and flying on July 1 was exactly thirty-nine days. In other words, the two periods matched. On a note of cautious triumph, Urner concluded that "this would tend to support the theory that the eggs were moved." All writings on the Short-eared Owl from this time forward would allude to this unusual behavior pattern, which Charlie Urner discovered in the Jersey Meadowlands.

The Short-eared Owl leads a life unusual in other ways, different from that of other members of the owl clan. So different, in fact, that you can almost believe that one night long ago a *protostrix* plunging through the dense familiarity of conifer forest took a wrong turn, followed an untraveled path, emerged into a clearing, and never looked back. The Short-eared Owl, *Asio flammeus*, tends to belie the notion that evolution is a straight tree with neatly pruned branches.

The Short-eared Owl is nearly fully diurnal—not merely crepuscular, which is to say, most active in the half-light of dusk and dawn, like some thirty of the world's 130 owl species, but as comfortable in the afternoon sunshine as other owls are in the shadows of night. The Short-eared hunts when it likes, naps at odd intervals, and in this way reverses the common order of owlish affairs: where most other owls are secretive and somber nocturnal birds, this one is outgoing and exuberant.

From this readaptation to daylight follow all kinds of other eccentricities. Whereas most owls' nocturnal habits are suited to the forest, the Short-eared is a bird of open spaces. It prefers the plains, delights in the marshes, and loves the gentle roll of sandy dunes. Open spaces have made the Short-eared perhaps the premier aerobat among owls. Short-eareds hunt with a light, airy touch. When great quiet holds the plains, the Short-eared is a carefree floater. When the winds are up, it glides with tremendous speed and skill.

Skimming low, effortlessly following the contour of the ground, the Short-eared takes advantage of every upcurrent. From full velocity it can brake to a sharp midair halt, flap once or twice, and hover, wavering this way and that, before lowering its talons and pouncing on its prey below. Sometimes this owl does not stop at all but swoops smoothly down, grasps the prey in its claws, and just as neatly lifts off again, sheering swiftly downwind for a quiet spot to devour its meal. The Short-eared can accomplish the wingflip and the forward somersault. When small birds mob it, the owl rotates on its back and fights with its talons pointed skyward. There is practically no end to what this owl can do with a hundred yards clear sailing and a puff of breeze. The Bog Trotter is the master of a thousand aerial maneuvers.

But of all the Short-eared's flying tricks, the most unique is also the one that sets it apart as the Romeo of owls—the amazing spring courtship display known as the "fluttering flag." The dance begins with the male owl rising, wheeling up and up in exceptionally slow, easy curves. For music, he accompanies himself in a bass monotone of rapid, melodious toots. Once he's attained great elevation, sometimes as high as fifteen hundred feet, where no prospective mate on the ground could possibly miss his performance, his sunlit wings lift high above him, and he pauses. Now he commences short, slanting dives, each ending in a graceful, upward swoop. Each time he streaks downward, he brings his wings together beneath his body and strikes them rapidly together with clapping strokes. Slanting up again, he lifts his wings and makes a new, lower, rasher dive, for the daring part of the display is when the male comes hurtling down with such velocity—and apparent recklessness—that a crash landing seems certain. Then, just at the last moment, he pulls out. These mad, passionate dives are always accompanied by wing-beating below, which one observer described as sounding like a flag fluttering in a stiff wind and another compared to "applauding his own performance." But there is no vanity involved: the fluttering flag is done to stir the hearts of marshy ladies. And it drives female owls to distraction. When the male owl finally lands, to nuzzle and preen, the female is seduced. After copulation, they wing up together, a pair of gay blades cutting capers, and the dance ends in an amorous chase over the moors. What makes the Short-eared Owl's courtship flight fascinating from a behavioral point of view is that the sound of the male's wing-clapping gives every appearance of a rehearsed, purposeful negation of the adaptation of silent flight. It is as if the Short-eared is communicating that his mating instinct has superseded his hunting instinct.

In all these marvelous maneuvers—in the wounded-bird ruse, but most of all in the sensuous courtship dance—the Short-eared Owl has raised the art of flight to new creative heights. If bodies have a language of their own, the wings of this Bog Trotter speak in love sonnets.

# T H R E E

I took a trip to Urner country, hoping to see the Short-eared's dance. Dawn was breaking over the Jersey Meadowlands as I drove through the Lincoln Tunnel. The sky paled rapidly to dishrag gray. I headed south on Route 1, past chemical plants and truck depots, sooty brick sweatshops, and tank-car sidings. Turning off the highway, I got lost in a maze of unmarked roads and dead-end alleys. Finally, I found a railroad trestle and entered a rutted, unpaved lane leading back through a colony of deteriorating warehouses, to a parking lot at the edge of the Meadowlands. On foot, I followed the railroad tracks until I came to a large outcrop of grimy schist. A police car was parked there on the gravel road between the north and south tracks, its engine running. The windows were all steamy. I rubbed away the windshield dew and peered in. A cop was sound asleep, cradling his pumpgun. Ahead lay a muddy track circling a hummock mounded high with garbage. Beyond the dump I could see the smooth expanse of phragmites stretching a mile or more to where the New Jersey Turnpike bisected the meadows. A dented white gas guzzler rolled ominously out of the reeds, perhaps having made some dawn delivery.

At the top of the outcrop was a grove of white birch saplings and the remains of a hoboes' camp: ashes, torn plastic tarp, empty tins. On the eastern slope was another grove, this one of stunted beech. Cottontail rabbits scattered through the undergrowth, and two robins zoomed through

in chase. At the top of a beech, a brilliant scarlet cardinal
sent out his forlorn mating call. In the leaves below, a towhee scratched the earth for something to eat. Flickers darted
through the trees, white rumps undulating, and redwinged
blackbirds sang their morning greetings. I stood at the summit and looked out over miles of spewing chimneys, traffic
jams, oil refineries, garbage piles. The sunlight seeped over
the New York City skyline like a hemorrhage.

I spent the rest of the day tramping the Meadowlands in
the slim hope of flushing a nesting Short-eared. It's tough
going in the Jersey meadows now, but not because the mud
is deep, nor because the sun is hot, nor the cattails thick.
It's tough going now because whole sectors are closed off by
chain-link fences with the red skull and crossbones. HAZARD,
the metal signs say: TOXIC WASTES. You have to circle the
perimeter and try to make your way through the slick, vis-
cous marl, only to find your way blocked again and again by
rusting coveys of hundred-gallon barrels oozing greasy, black
and copper-colored matter.

Beyond the waste dumps, hidden in the reeds, was an
even more ghastly sight: a heap of animal carcasses rotting
in the noonday sun. Decapitated deer, dead dogs with their
dorsal sides slashed and their guts hanging out, bloated cats
with their faces contorted in the anguished expressions of
death. The stink of putrid flesh was almost unbearable.
There were tiny green blowflies feeding everywhere. I
thought for a moment of some secret laboratory, of some
occult religious sect. I thought of death squads like those in
Central America, only specializing in animals, and then I got
so nauseous I stopped imagining an explanation and staggered away the same way I'd staggered in.

Later on, I came to a ghost town of abandoned brick
factories and corrugated-metal warehouses set among the

reeds. The ghost-factory windows had been scrupulously shot out, one by one. The floors were littered with glass shards and strewn with moldy papers from overturned metal file cabinets. Huge pieces of dead machinery lay on the floors in pools of oil. The wind whistled, and the tin sliding doors, drawn back, banged against the walls. I climbed the stairs to the attics, where pigeon droppings and metal tailings coated the splintered floorboards. There was no way to say for certain what the ghost factories had once produced. Whatever it was, we no longer needed it or wanted it, or perhaps we make it better or cheaper someplace else.

The only owl I saw was an imaginary one: it stared out with great, dark, accusatory eyes.

# F O U R

In 1904, when Charlie Urner graduated from the University of Wisconsin and came home to work for his family's New York market-reporting firm, the New Jersey Meadowlands were still largely undeveloped—a no-man's land in the best sense of that term. Elizabeth, Hackensack, Bayonne, and Rahway were small, residential towns bordering untrampeled moors. On summer Sundays, the immigrant workers of New York and Newark would board trains for the meadows to take the sun and breathe the fresh air, released for a few hours from the sordid, stifling heat of the big city. The New Jersey meadows formed the western part of an even vaster wetland belt on New York City's southern reach. East across Newark Bay, you could see on Staten Island the terminus reached by the last glacier of the Great Ice Age, slicing across the island like a geological Mason-Dixon Line. On the northern side, the glacier had deposited its moraine, the boulders and gravels carried along in its icy paws. The terrain here was jagged and hilly, as if caressed by a huge iron rake. South of the glacial drift were flat, sandy lowlands dotted with the first stands of scrub pine, stands that stretched south all the way to the New Jersey Pine Barrens. Here, in Staten Island's lowlands, the marshes continued the march they'd begun in the New Jersey meadows. Across the Verrazano Narrows, they resumed through lower Brooklyn, crossed the hundreds of islets and peninsulas of brackish Jamaica Bay, before coming to an end in the sandy dunes of

Long Island's barrier beaches. All told, this distance of some thirty miles was excellent Short-eared Owl habitat. The long stretch of wetlands marked the transitional zone between the sweeter, milder climate of the central seaboard and the sterner weather of New England. As such, the wetlands served—and still serve to some extent—as a favorite wintering haven for ducks and geese, as well as an important stopover for a tremendous variety of shorebirds and waders on their annual migrations. Directly in the migration route known as the Atlantic flyway, where millions of birds must venture each spring and autumn, the ponds and inlets hidden in the reeds provided food and cover. In those days, the marshlands teemed with small mammals, reptiles, fish, and crustaceans. Charlie Urner could record a hundred species of birds in a single day.

He resettled in his native New Jersey, commuting to Manhattan, where he worked as a reporter for the Urner-Barry Company's *Producers' Price-Current*, a trade paper furnishing wholesale quotations from the dairy, vegetable, meat, and poultry markets. But his chief work and pleasure was showing others the bird life of his beloved Meadowlands. He became president of the New York Linnaean Society, board member of New Jersey Audubon, leader of the New Jersey Field Ornithology Club, and sponsor of the Passaic and Raritan Valleys Ornithological Club, later renamed The Urner Club in his honor. For many years he led the Christmas birdcount at Barnegat Light. Not satisfied with this annual census, Urner created a spring version of the event known as the "Big Day," which has since become a tradition among keen birdwatchers. He was one of the country's leading authorities on the Short-eared Owl, the only owl species specifically adapted to the open lowlands of Charlie Urner's native haunts. In his notebooks was the evidence of the contributions dedicated amateurs can make to the natural sciences. Charlie Urner suffered heart failure and died on the evening of June 22, 1938, while driving home from the Linnaean Society's special summer meeting.

By that time, however, change was coming to the New Jersey meadows, not in single spies, but in battalions. The comparatively cheap real estate close to New York City was simply too tempting to those who consider open wetlands "empty" wastelands. The New Jersey Turnpike, now a national symbol of industrial blight, opened the meadows to manufacturing and heavy trucking. Later, Newark International Airport would be built, and then the Meadowlands Sports Complex. The meadowlands became the dumping grounds of the northeast. Meanwhile, the lowlands of Staten Island and Brooklyn were filled for housing developments, shopping malls, and beltways—all except the lands set aside to serve as New York's two active garbage dumps and the islands in Jamaica Bay, which were, after a strenuous battle by conservationists, protected as a federal wildlife refuge. For the rest, only small pockets of the wetlands remain, continually shrinking each time developers take another bite. Wherever we have left a niggardly patch of earth unmolested, nature rushes in hungrily, filling it with life. But as these pockets became fewer and farther apart, flora and fauna crowded there in a turmoil of species, competing for space and survival.

Instead of creating arks to save creatures, we created a new type of ghetto for plants and animals: nature ghettos. As in human ghettos, the strong and the selfish survive, the fragile and nonconforming perish. The shy trillium and gentle columbine are rubbed out by the slick poison ivy and tough chicory. The sweet-voiced warblers are muscled aside by the sleazy starlings. At length, phragmites blanketed the marsh pockets, choking out most other plant life. They have proved by far the most tenacious of all local plants, ready to invade any vacant lot or send up shoots between buildings. All you see today are the phragmites' soulless stalkheads, bending to the breezes. Unfortunately, the phragmites, which are capable of providing cover for birds, also provide an excellent screen for junking cars, tossing garbage, dumping toxic wastes, and depositing stiffs—gangland as well as animal. These activities render most of the remnant wetlands feculent. Charlie Urner would feel out of place among the hoods in cars, driving around the marshes leaving presents.

The trail of the Short-eared Owl pointed east toward Staten Island. There, just before dark, I met two local birders, Al and Mike, who agreed to spend a summer evening going for owls. Al was a sallow thirty-year-old working guy, a bus driver with a ginger mustache and muttonchop sideburns, driving a dented, olive-drab Dodge. He started birdwatching three years ago, and soon became such a fanatic that he brings his binoculars to work with him. If he sees something good on his route, he stops the bus. He has memorized the passerines' songs. Now he's taking a college correspondence course in ecology. Perhaps Charlie Urner would have liked Al. Mike was a local high-school hotshot in a nylon windbreaker with the word *Mike* embroidered on the pocket. He came geared for an expedition to the Tikal—zoom field-glasses, camera, flashlight, and large tape deck. "I took a tape of Barred Owl off the Roger Tory Peterson records," he said.

"Are there nesting records of Barred Owls on Staten Island?" I asked him.

"Not for a hundred years!" He laughed.

We pulled out of the shopping mall parking lot. Al said, "We really haven't got the best territory around here for owls, it's all been pretty much developed. But there's a barge sitting down in the Arthur Kill where I saw a Barn Owl two or three weeks ago."

"Let's go for it," I said.

On the way, I pumped Al for information. It was two
weeks back, he'd been out birding with his wife, and it was
still twilight. The Barn Owl had scooted out of the old barge
tied up in the Kill below an iron highway bridge. A Barn Owl
had also been recorded in the same spot during Staten Island's annual Christmas birdcount, so it was apparently not
a newcomer to the area. When we got to the iron bridge,
we parked off the road in the phragmites and slid down the
garbage-strewn slope about fifteen feet to the edge of the
Kill. The dilapidated barge sat on the bottom of the stagnant
channel. The place looked like the cover of a John Steinbeck
novel, with glaring sodium arc spotlights lighting the scummy
water, rust red and slime green. A foul smell came up off
that water, part chemical, part vegetable, and in large part
raw sewage. The iron bridge vibrated heavily with each passing car, but when semis went over the bridge sounded like
it would collapse. The Kill wound back along the edge of a
tremendous dump—"largest solid landfill in the U.S.," Mike
noted, not without a hint of local pride. He said the people
who lived in the vicinity complained of headaches and
chronic respiratory ailments, associated with PCBs and other
toxics dumped into the landfill. The wastes leached out as
ground water into the Kill. A local TV news reporter had
stood in almost this very spot and proclaimed it "the most
poisoned place in America." The rate of bowel cancers here,
I found out later, was five to ten times the national norm. It
did not seem a nice neighborhood for an owl to raise a family.

Yet no sooner did we reach the edge of the Kill than we
heard a bizarre falsetto shriek—"Kek-kek-kek-kek-kek-kek-
kek!"—repeated twenty-three times. Then a phantasmic
white form emerged from the shadow of the bridge. Without
flapping once, the monkey-faced owl sailed past on the far
side of the barge, out into the blackness over the dump.

"There it goes!" cried Al, with as much wonder as pride in having led us here.

We hid behind the rotted pilings to wait. Sure enough, exactly fifteen minutes later the white owl floated in, fast and low, carrying a small prey item in its talons, and swiftly disappeared into the shadows under the bridge. No sooner had it vanished, however, than another owl emerged from the same spot and headed out. This one, too, kept to the far side of the barge, so all we could see was the white form flitting by for little more than a second. With the two owls taking hunting shifts like that, it was evident they had young in a nest under the bridge. I began to clock the time it took them to leave, catch prey, and return, thinking all the while of a favorite passage in Gilbert White, in which, speaking of the "white owls" of Selbourne, he said, "I have minuted these birds with my watch for an hour together, and have found that they return to their nests, the one or the other of them, about once in five minutes; reflecting at the same time on the adroitness that every animal is possessed of as regards the well-being of itself and offspring." The Barn Owls under the Staten Island bridge, I'm afraid, didn't do as well, averaging more like thirteen minutes. But considering what they were up against in that dismal environment, I could conclude with a clear conscience that our modern Barn Owls are every bit as adroit as those of Gilbert White's day.

Out in the distant darkness over the dump, we could hear the owl cackling: "Keeeeeeeeee-ek? Keeeeeeeeeee-ek?" To which its mate back at the nest would respond with a falsetto ending in a gargle: "Peep-peep-peep-peep-peep-ahhhhhh!"

Barn Owls let out these ghoulish wails while hunting, but nobody knows why. Some think they may do it to frighten mice to death, thereby allowing the owl to conserve the energy that might be spent chasing them down. Others think the weird calls are territorial declarations, but the cries could also communicate to mate and young that food has been located and is on the way. In this case, though, I felt fairly sure that the pair were making alarm calls, set off by our presence. I wanted to lead my cohorts away and not disturb the owls: what with the clang and din of traffic, the spotlights, and the reek of toxics, I figured this *Tyto* family had quite enough problems. They might well have been the last pair of nesting Barn Owls on Staten Island, for all I knew, and it would be a shame to create additional disturbance. So we called it a night, and I went east again, to the Brooklyn side of the Narrows.

The Fountain Avenue Dump in Brooklyn was not the most refreshing place to spend a summer afternoon birdwatching. An endless procession of trucks rumbled through, and the monster earthmovers shoved the waste up into mountains that grew before your eyes, hundreds of feet high. Here and there, smoky fires burned, and the noise was deafening and the dust choking. I walked the perimeter for a few hours looking for any sign of owl, but saw instead a glossy ibis, which was at least a fair consolation prize. I was heading back to the car near the weighing station when I heard a human "Who-whoo!" and turned to meet a smiling, well-tanned young sanitation engineer in a hard hat. "Looking for owls, right?" he said.

"Right. Seen any?"

"They're over at the Edgemere Dump in Rockaway, one dump down. They were here last year, hanging around in the lower dump area. But then we altered the disposal pattern—what I mean is, we bulldozed the garbage from one place to another, the one near where the owls were hanging around. I haven't seen 'em since."

"What sort were they, could you tell?"

"I dunno the name," he said. "But they didn't have any necks at all. When they flew, they looked just like a flying cigar."

"Did they fly close to the ground?"

"Yup."

"During the day?"

"Yup."

"Did they settle on the ground, or in trees?"

"The ground—ain't no trees here."

"How many were there?"

"A bunch of them together. Six, or eight, maybe."

"Sounds like Short-eared Owls," I said. "What time of year was it?"

"Late winter. They hung around the dump all winter, then they finally moved over to Edgemere. I seen 'em over there, and also another bird—big, long legs, pointy bill, mean looking."

"Dark patch on its head?"

"Yup."

"Night heron, probably."

"Mean looking, right?"

"I'm only interested in owls." It sounded like they'd had a family of Short-eareds that had found good hunting in the dump and stayed together through the winter, or possibly a group of yearling birds that had kept company over the winter before seeking out territory and mates in the spring.

The engineer said, "All you got here now is the wild dogs back there, and the rats. I keep an eye out for the birds. It's fun. Go over to Edgemere, that's where to see 'em. Ask for Bill."

"I'll do that. Thanks for the briefing."

"Good luck," he said.

# S  E  V  E  N

At the Edgemere Dump, on a spit of land in Far Rockaway, the garbage of New York City is bulldozed into immense, flat plateaus, with a network of rutted lanes running through. An oily breeze wafts off Jamaica Bay, and the hot, greasy smell of rotting food gets into your nostrils and into your pores. For reasons unknown, there are men guarding the garbage, as if it were a precious commodity. They lead as solitary an existence as any desert ascetic, staying far back in their scrap tin shanties, with only the incessant oily winds for company. Working the Gehenna of the urban world does have one compensation, though, which is that you get to know the wildlife—feral dogs, stray cats, sea gulls, flies, rats, and, of course, the owls that come hunting the rodents. The men who work the garbage plains have something vaguely feral about them, too.

He insisted his name was "Beel," not Bill. I found him leaving his shack at dusk, but he didn't want a ride, he preferred to walk—by himself, he said. His skin was swarthy as that of a king of Araby, his shoulder-length hair hung in mousy, lardy mats. A black mole clung to his cheek like a tattoo, and his eyes gave the impression of spinning nervously, like pinwheels. It was hard to get him to talk: he didn't expect to see another human here. But when I persevered, he grudgingly relented, and muttered what he knew in hushed tones.

"Yeah, I seen 'em. Two Saturdays ago. A pair on 'em. It

was just getting light, in the morning. I musta skeered 'em. They was together, the two on 'em. I seen 'em together before here. They took off when they seen me coming. Flew back there, by the water. You go back that way, you might see 'em. Maybe they got a nest back there, I ain't looked. Way far back there, that's where you got to go."

"Anything else you remember?"

He gazed away. "Nothing else. They screamed when they flew away, that's all."

"They what?"

"They screamed."

"Short-eared Owls don't usually scream when they fly," I mused out loud. "Unless they've got a nest nearby. I thought you had Short-eareds out here."

"Who told you that?" he demanded to know. "I don't know what the hell kind they are. Look, I gotta go now."

"Please, just one more question. What color were these owls?"

"White owls," he said, "They was all white."

Barn Owls—not Short-eareds, after all! I let Beel go, drove around to the other side of the bay, and in ten minutes located a big abandoned house. The ground outside was ankle deep in Barn Owl pellets. I was crawling around on my knees inspecting them with my flashlight when the police arrived.

"—The hell do you think you're doing?" said the cop.

"No problem, officer." I rose with my hands up. "You see, um, I'm from the Audubon Society. We had a report of Short-eared Owls out here. But it's nothing to worry about, it's only Barn Owls."

The cop looked at me rather strangely, but after a moment he decided it was all right to ask, "Hey, is it really true owls can fly without making noise?"

I went home, took a long shower to scrub the filth of the rubbish pits away, and decided the question was this: if Short-eared Owls no longer breed around New York, where do they go to court, mate, and nest in the summer? Afterward, I went to the library and checked every reference I could find on *Asio flammeus*, searching for a new lead. Here are some incidental curiosities concerning the Bog Trotter's behavior I picked up along the way.

∽ Lewis Wayne Walker tells the story of once working the Flushing Meadows outside New York City during duckhunting season, when the alarm calls of a small-bird mob drew his attention to a badly wounded Short-eared. The bird was crouching in a clump of cattails with a crippled wing. Intending to return for the owl later, Walker covered it with an old crab trap he found in the marsh grasses and went on his way. When he came back a few hours later, Walker flushed a healthy owl, which buzzed his head, then flew away. The second owl had been hunting for its imprisoned mate: on top of the crab trap Walter found a meadow mouse, a Norway rat, and a red-winged blackbird, all neatly laid out for the captive owl, like delicacies on a sushi board. Walker commented that it would not have been so extraordinary to find an owl feeding its entrapped mate or offspring, except that this was autumn, the season of migration and dispersal, not of nesting and monogamy. Family feeling was supposed to have been mothballed, not to resume until the following spring. "A strange example of the devotion of one owl to another," Walker concluded.

꙳ Short-eared Owls apparently have a yen to see the world. No one is quite sure about their movements, either seasonal or in the span of life, so a number of terms are used to describe them. Some authorities call the Short-eared Owl "very migratory." Others term them "wanderers," or "migrating regularly and irregularly." The Bog Trotter that shows up in a place he's never been sighted before is called an "accidental," but my favorite term is the one applied to the owl that stays here a few days, moves on to greener marshes, and later goes somewhere else again. They call these owls "vagrants." Whatever term is used, it describes the fact that Short-eared Owls often turn up in places other owls don't. According to one old record, a Short-eared landed on a steamship in the Atlantic. The passengers who rushed to the foredeck to view the strange visitor remarked that it didn't look particularly tired but, on the contrary, rather calm, collected, and curious. After hitching a short ride, the globe trotter took off again for parts unknown. At the time, the steamer was eight hundred miles from the nearest landfall.

꙳ The owls of dark forests and secluded graveyards may be loners, but not the Short-eared. Our Bog Trotter enjoys company and makes friends easily, particularly with a certain member of the hawk family with whom the owl competes for food and territory. This is the marsh hawk, or hen harrier, the handsome glider often seen skimming over stubble fields and plains, "slow as the gates of spring," as one poet put it. Many people, including Lewis

Walker on a field trip with Charlie Urner, have mistaken the one bird for the other, so similar are their patterns of flight, though their field markings are easily distinguishable. The owl is blunt in profile and more round-faced, with a short tail and buff patches under the wings. The harrier has somewhat owlish facial disks but a bright white rump patch before long tail feathers. The female harrier is a comely reddish cinnamon color, while the smaller male is a gray bird, sometimes called blue.

The reason the two species are often confused is that, although completely unrelated to each other, they share the same habitat, their hunting territories sometimes actually overlap, and they seem to somehow divide up the available prey with an unusual degree of social tolerance. During nesting season, marsh hawk and Short-eared Owl sometimes nest close to one another in a display of avian neighborliness, as though the two predators have a pact not to depredate each other's nests. Undocumented reports tell of finding marsh hawk chicks in owl nests and vice versa. In his outstanding book *The Hen Harrier*, British ornithologist Donald Watson describes something equally intimate. Harriers are known to roost communally in winter—usually in family groups—and ornithologists observing these roosts have noted Short-eared Owls landing there. The owls arrive at sunup for their early-morning nap, just at the hour when the harriers are spreading over the fields in search of breakfast. But sometimes, should the owls come early or the hawks leave late, the Short-eared set down before the harriers have gone. Then the two mighty birds of prey peacefully share a common roost. The two species stand side by side, like chums outside a factory gate, schmoozing at the change of shifts.

∽ There is an old Latin American legend, perhaps apocryphal, about how Short-eared Owls saved the city of Buenos Aires from ruin. The coypu is a common rodent of the pampas, rat-shaped but somewhat larger, with bright red incisors. Beneath its long, coarse hair is a layer of fine brown fur, which used to be exported to Europe. Once, because of the coypu's value as a furbearer, the dictator Rosas issued a decree making the killing of coypus a criminal offense. As a result, the rodents multiplied wildly, left their native pampas, migrated to the city, and swarmed everywhere in search of food. The rodent plague threatened civil order, but then, suddenly and mysteriously, Short-eared Owls filled the skies by the hundreds. Working with cooperation and efficiency, the owls quickly put down the infestation. Within a few days, the coypu was nearly extinct.

This story, a modern version of the Pied Piper of Hamelin, might be completely unbelievable but for the fact that similar owl counterattacks are definitely recorded. During the great plague of field mice that occurred in the farmlands of northern England in 1890, four hundred pairs of owls appeared in the stricken area. Another rodent plague in the Fresno, California, agricultural valley, in 1913, was suppressed only when owls arrived in force. Unfortunately, during the Fresno plague, ignorant farmers shot a number of Short-eareds before realizing they were killing their own saviors. The obvious moral: birds of prey should be rigorously protected as the first step during any rodent outbreak.

∽ In an old number of *Audubon* magazine, I finally found the reference to the Short-eared Owl's nesting range I was looking for. It was contained in a life history of the bird written by Edward Howe Forbush, Massachusetts State Ornithologist in the 1920s, and an eminence in his field. In one place, Forbush wrote, "On the rolling hills of Nantucket and on the bushy plains of Martha's Vineyard, I have watched with delight [the Short-eared Owl's] daylight hunting, or have had three or four at a time floating erratically about me in the dusk of early evening." He also said, "[The Short-eared] nests on the dry plains of Martha's Vineyard in the heath hen country and on sandy islands in the sea, where there is no fresh water."

Forbush's word was good enough for me. I closed the books and headed north for Martha's Vineyard.

It was the end of a sublime July day, one of those days that probably occur only on islands, only in summer, and only after a storm front has passed through, leaving the atmosphere clear and tranquil. The sky was so lucid you could watch the ospreys for hours as they soared the upper thermals. The sun, no longer crimson as before the storm, broke stark lemon over the sea, casting a brilliant glint that lasted throughout the day. And the ocean, its fury spent for the time being, stirred briefly, then fell back, still and smooth as glass. The noon doldrums brought a speckling of high oatmeal clouds, wispy and barely moving. By afternoon everything was suffused in lambent light, heat, and languor. The drooping saw grasses twirled lazy rings in the sand, first clockwise, then counterclockwise, like sundials that couldn't make up their minds, until finally they gave up all movement completely.

The day seemed to drift by, like an oarless boat carried on a slow current. The dunes, the tidal ponds beyond them, and the sea and sky themselves, stretched into vivid, bold stripes until late afternoon, when the accumulated heat, rising in waves, blurred all distinctions in a softened haze. For a long time, the sun refused to set, perching cadmium orange over the low scrub hills in the west, which gradually turned a cool forest green. The only sounds were the lulling crash of distant breakers and the whistle of swans' wings as the birds moved in great flocks seeking cover for the night ahead.

On this day I went hunting for the Short-eared Owl's nest on Martha's Vineyard, which is probably better known as a posh summer resort than an island deposit of glacial moraine off the Massachusetts coast, containing some of the finest heath and tidal marsh for harrier and Short-eared Owl nesting on the east coast. All afternoon I'd worked east, from South Pond to Chilmark Great Pond to Black Point Pond, in a borrowed rowboat, making use of the narrow connecting inlets left behind when the sea flooded over the barrier beaches. The ponds were extremely shallow, but the tiny boat drew next to nothing; where it could go no farther, I put on hip waders and searched every quarter on foot, pond after pond, marsh after marsh, plain after plain. It was the kind of day that inspires a birder to greater and greater effort, because even if you don't find what you set out after, the season is so ripe and the weather is so fine that you inevitably get into all sorts of delightful situations.

My list for the day already included a pair of green herons, a pair of yellow-crowned night herons, a dozen snowy egrets, and osprey that had swooped down within fifty feet of the boat, and an American bittern stalking shellfish from a sandbar. When, around five o'clock, I sighted a female harrier hunting slowly over the scrub, I knelt down in the boat and let it drift into the tules to get a closer look. She was a large and magnificent bird, floating with her wings fully extended, her color a reddish shade of brown that reminded me of some lightly oiled tropical wood. As I drew closer, I could observe the way she used her bar tail like a rudder, half spreading and tilting it side to side to balance or adjust her course. Down she'd dip below the trees, then up she'd rise, her arcs quite musical and fluid. And then she was joined by her smaller, gray mate, not her equal in plumage but equally agile. They flowed east together, more like energy than matter. A few hundred yards east, they vanished below low scrub. Assuming they'd struck prey, I rose to my knees and paddled with one oar in their direction. Some birders take pride in not being "chasers," but as far as I'm concerned it's hot pursuit or nothing: every time you watch a bird there's a chance of picking up some new bit of behavior, achieving some new insight, framing some new question. More than anything, however, it's a matter of temperament and insatiable curiosity: I'd never seen harriers eating before. Did they pluck the prey's feathers first? Did they share the food with each other?

The next time I saw them, however, they'd landed on a small pitch pine only two hundred feet or so from a summer cottage—and the tree held not two but three marsh hawks. A family! I rejoiced at my luck, partly because confirmation of harriers successfully nesting is a positive indication that Short-eared Owls will also be breeding in the vicinity— though, of course, not a sure sign. The young harrier was fully fledged, and almost as big as its father, but with immature plumage colored much like its mother's. I had paddled and drifted to within a hundred yards of their perch, a distance that is practically nothing to the sharp eyes of a hawk. I felt sure they were aware of my presence, yet the adult harriers showed no sign of alarm. On the contrary, after staring quite calmly in my direction, preening and rousing her feathers, the female harrier hopped down from the topmost branch and nudged her offspring off the limb into flight, as if to say, "Show the nice man how well you fly."

The young hawk performed a neat loop and returned to its proud parents. This was as close as one was likely to get to observing that crucial point in a raptor's development in which instincts are shaped into definite behavioral traits. What can the young bird of prey do on its own, and how much do the parents teach it? Do the parents actually transmit information about, say, what height to cruise while hunting, how to dive and attack? Or, does the fledgling learn by observing its elders and playing follow the leader? Or, again, does learning to become a bird of prey proceed by trial and error, with the family providing a protective, secure, educational environment, demonstrating approval when the young bird does it right—or goading it into activity should it show any timidity? It's a fascinating business, and, entranced by the free demonstration, I lost track of time and let the afternoon slip away.

The sun was already balanced on the horizon when I started back for the landing. The swans were moving in flocks hundreds strong, the crows gathering for their nightly family quarrel. Way over to the west, an osprey was silhouetted at the top of an artificial nesting platform, somnolent, not a feather stirring. A mosquito hatch rose over the still water. I set my back to the oars, and small whirlpools gurgled and swirled in the boat's wake. Then a mosquito caught me on the hand, another on the neck. I rowed faster, but they caught up with little trouble. They were biting my back through the shirt, humming in my ears and around my head. I rowed, if not for my life then for my sanity, because these relentless little monsters can drive people crazy. There was no hope of rowing faster than the insects could fly. The best I could hope for was that my exertions would create a small false breeze that might deter them from landing. But pull as I might they were completely unimpressed. I was stroking like someone possessed, shaking my head frantically, jerking my shoulders, stamping my feet against the boat's bottom. They seemed to like that, and kept coming, swarming, so there was nothing left but to shout useless curses into the silent dusk and try to keep going. Rowing the last few hundred yards, I was idiotically slapping the oars on the water's surface so that the splash would drive off the invidious bloodsuckers. I got completely soaked in the process, but there was a joyless satisfaction in seeing a few of their host thrown to the bottom of the boat, stunned by the spray.

Fifty yards to go, and the only thing on my mind was hitting shore and dashing for my tent across the fields. The bow scraped bottom, I grabbed my daypack. As I leaped ashore waving both arms wildly over my head, I happened to look up—and a Short-eared Owl was directly above, waving back with its wings.

It had already grown too dark to make out the bird's color or features, but in the even indigo dusk its silhouette was unmistakable. Blunt-nosed, stubby-tailed, a flying cigar with incredibly long, pointed wings working back and forth irregularly, somewhat awkwardly. It was hard to say which of us was more surprised—the owl, which had probably recently emerged from roost to hunt when it came across this madman at the shoreline flinging himself about in the mellow evening, or I, who had spent weeks and traveled hundreds of miles on the trail of this bird, only to meet up with it in the midst of a fearsome mosquito attack, when it was already dark and I'd given up for the day. Such is the owler's lot: you sometimes get the impression that owls choose the conditions of rendezvous.

My field notebook entry of that evening continues: "At the moment I saw it, only about fifteen feet away and as many high, the owl's wings were pumping in order to hover over the ground, just up the low bank behind me. At the same time, its talons came down, and stretched wide. In fact, I'd caught the owl in the precise moment of beginning its attack, but when it saw me, the bird simply veered away, retracting its claws, and with a few pumps of its wings, sped off over the field, neither rising nor dipping, yet tilting side to side as it slipped further into the dusk. I raced up the bank in time to see a rabbit thumping for its run in the salt hay: the intended victim, no doubt."

# E L E V E N

For five days I combed the island's heaths and marshes, by boat and on foot, not finding the Short-eared Owl's nest, but discovering what the owl was up against here. At Katama— Forbush's "ancient hunting grounds"—the dunes were newly crisscrossed with trails tramped down by tourists and sunbathers heading toward the beaches. Their cars were parked in the sand, along ditches, in the fields, by the hundreds. Along the beach road, dozens of new deck houses for summer residents, some tacky, some splendid, converted formerly open areas to developed lots, putting new pressure on the remaining habitat.

I ended each afternoon on a dune rise, where nothing blocked the view across panels of low furze and high, fine-grained sky. Immense rush-hour flights were in motion, birds stacked up, stretched out, streaking forward. I stood guard for an hour or two, studying each speck in the air for its profile and characteristic flight, checking with my field-glasses those that soared, undulated, wavered, or hovered— in short, any with suspiciously owly movements. After sundown, I made for cover—a stream bank rank with green grasses, a pine grove, or the skeleton of an old fishing vessel sunk in the sand. Squatting down there, I remained as still as possible until the last glow of day drained from the sky, hoping the chance might bring a dancing owl overhead since conscientious effort seemed to be failing. But although I counted nine harriers, only one more Short-eared appeared, again cruising rapidly by just at twilight.

Past nightfall, backtracking through dirt lanes walled snugly by dense scrub oak, I kept crossing paths with skunks, their amber eyeshine flaming in my flashlight. They stood in the road like brazen highwaymen, not giving an inch until I tossed sand or pebbles, then slinking off nonchalantly. Skunks, as it happens, compete for mice, the staple of the Short-eared Owl's diet. Skunks and raccoons also like bird eggs for dinner. Both ground predators were in such abundance that I couldn't help but think that many birds' nests must be destroyed.

# T W E L V E

By inhabiting open country, the Short-eared Owl has spread over a tremendous range—in fact, the bird has been found on every continent but Antarctica. By not waiting for night-fall, the Short-eared has developed into the owl family's most sensational flier, with complex ritual flights expressive of love, sport, and parental sacrifice. By building its own nest, boldly moving its eggs, and uniting in cooperative spirit when farmlands are endangered by rodent plagues, the Short-eared has shown its distinctive personality, as well as making itself one of the most useful of all birds to man.

Yet there is still another rare quality of the Short-eared Owl and that is the number of eggs the female lays each year. Some authorities claim from three to seven. W. H. Hudson said, "The eggs are three or four, white, nearly spherical." Whatever number is accepted, the remarkable thing is that the clutch is so small.

Generally, the size of a bird's egg clutch depends on three factors. The first, and least understood, is food availability. In so-called "rodent years," when prey is abundant, female owls tend to lay more eggs. In lean prey years they tend to lay fewer. No one knows the physiological mechanism by which this natural form of birth control works, but it is a well-documented pattern, and increases the chances of the offsprings' survival. It is also the main way that the prey population itself exerts control over the predator population. The second factor, better understood, is the species' own size and puissance. As a rule, large and powerful birds lay fewer eggs. Great Horned Owls, for example, don't need huge clutches, because few creatures have the strength and courage to rob a Great Horned's nest. Finally, birds nesting in relatively vulnerable places tend to lay more eggs than birds that spend time and effort choosing secure nest sites. Cliffs, caves, and high trees are relatively safe. Open ground is, of course, most vulnerable, and many ground nesters lay enormous clutches. Bobwhite quail, for example, lay fourteen or fifteen eggs. Pheasants lay up to eighteen. The Short-eared Owl is a ground nester, but lays only four or five, or perhaps six eggs. To be sure, the Short-eared Owl is not as defenseless as the quail. But to nest in the path of floods, scythes, and skunks, and to make only half a dozen eggs, does seem to put an unusual degree of trust in the ultimate benevolence of nature. Perhaps only a reckless bird would let the fate of the species ride on the number six—or perhaps it's an evolutionary flaw. But I prefer to interpret it as an act of faith in the future, a daring statement of hope: the Short-eared Owl challenges next year to be better than last, and tells us that life, after all, is a game optimists can sometimes win.

# T H I R T E E N

"As for your Short-eared Owl, I can almost guarantee you won't find them breeding on the island at this time," said Augustus Ben David, the naturalist at the Vineyard's Felix Neck Wildlife Sanctuary. "Just a few years back, they were frequent breeders. Why, you'd drive down in Katama, or Chappaquiddick, and see them right along the roadside. They'd be all over the place. Out here at Felix Neck, in the early seventies, you'd always have Short-eared Owls working the dunes. Nowadays when an owl is sighted, it's a major event and gets written up in *The Vineyard Gazette* birding column. That's how rare they've become."

We were sitting on the house deck in the full sweep of the noonday sun, where Gus Ben David was keeping a protective eye on the light of his life, a yearling osprey he'd handraised in the hope of returning it to the wild state. The osprey perched on its hacking box thirty feet away in the back yard, but from where I sat it faced me directly over Gus's shoulder, and it was remarkable how the man and his bird resembled each other. The osprey had a square, stolid frame, the naturalist had a square, stolid frame. The bird had a short, slightly hooked beak, and so did Gus. Not to mention the solemn dignity that marked the demeanor of both. Such resemblances are not completely coincidental. Gus Ben David was dressed in the drab olive and neutral grays of a park service or ranger corps, the colors of facts, expertise, hard information. A Vineyard native in his late thirties, he is descended from the island's Portuguese sea-men, fishermen, and merchants, the same tough race that first discovered the New World. You would have no qualms about sailing into the unknown with Gus Ben David at the helm. You could rely on him to gauge the winds with skill, read the constellations, ascertain the safest route. His recom-mendations would be backed by painstaking study, common sense, and a steely can-do spirit. Self-taught and self-made, Gus specializes in raptors, and has trained birds for falconry. He is deeply involved in captive breeding for release, which is thought by some as the way to preserve endangered spe-cies. But the idea is not without its opponents. To those who argue that birds of prey raised in captivity are never really the same as birds raised by their parents—that there is simply too much for a young raptor to learn—the ambi-tious young working biologists of this generation might offer themselves as the best evidence: Gus Ben David has be-come what he is without family connections to pave his way.

A few hundred yards beyond us on the Neck, rising into the sky like Jack's beanstalk, was the sanctuary's wooden osprey stand, at the top of which stood a mated pair with their young of the year. Gus explained that he'd taken his yearling osprey from up there the previous summer. The mother had gotten herself caught in a plastic six-pack ring, and when Gus climbed the pole to free her, he'd found the chick completely mired in monofilament fishing line. "Os-preys are great junk collectors," he said. "A few days more and the mother would have got her talons caught in the line and pulled that whole nest over the edge of the pole. It would have been a real mess."

Gus Ben David brought the chick home and called it Mono. Soon he would see if the pole nest family would accept Mono, and perhaps teach the yearling how to hunt.

"What do you think has caused the owl's decline here?" I steered the conversation back.

"A number of factors have contributed," he said. "First comes habitat destruction. Development. If you've been down to Katama now and seen the building that's going on, well, that area was once all open marsh and dune. The Short-eared needs that open rolling country for hunting. So that's one. They need that broad, open terrain.

"And then, of course, there's the introduction of other predators, raccoon and skunk," Gus continued. "For years the island had no ground predators but the feral housecat. Then about twenty years ago, someone introduced skunks and raccoons. There are stories about who it was—a guy who kept exotic pets. A few escaped. Now? I mean, they are just all over.

"That was a very serious introduction. Offshore islands like this were important for having no mammalian predators. It allowed birds to breed in relative safety. On an island, you have a closed ecosystem, so any outside introduction is felt all the more. And to a degree, housing development makes an even larger predator population viable. The more houses and people, the more trash and garbage they put out, and since the raccoons and skunks can feed off the garbage, it falsely maintains a large population. That's what happens in an insular situation like this. An exotic predator is introduced into a vulnerable closed system and runs rampant. Personally, I wouldn't be adverse to—I hate to use the word 'bounty'—but some form of program to take the pressure off. These skunks and raccoons, they are just voracious."

I wondered out loud if the Short-eared was gone from the island forever.

"In nature," said Gus Ben David, "it's hard to put a definite answer as to why some things disappear. But in general things aren't getting better for the Short-eared Owl. I wouldn't say they'll never breed here again. If key and primary areas are maintained, they might make a comeback and nest on Martha's Vineyard again."

But Gus Ben David had no fondness for the big "ifs" of habitat preservation. We both knew the owl was competing for some of the most picturesque, desirable, and expensive shorefront property in the entire country. I left the island a few days later, convinced that if there were still Short-eared Owls nesting there, they were very few, they were sitting tighter than ever, and becoming more reclusive, perhaps returning during nesting season to a more nocturnal existence.

# F O U R T E E N

So the Short-eared Owl loses ground on the east coast, repaid for its iconoclastic behavior and the exquisite beauty of its ritual flights with the steady encroachment on its habitat. As a breeding bird, the Marsh Owl is already as rare in the industrial wastes of New Jersey as on the pleasure shores of New England. The lack of nesting success is usually a warning sign of a species in trouble. The slippage the bird is suffering, however, comes about as a result of what are, for us, ordinary economic processes. These processes of expansion, development, and construction are rapidly banishing from our midst many of the life forms in the higher vertebrate classes that are nature's true masterpieces.

It's not known how many owls there are in the United States. No base line of population statistics exists against which to measure their abundance or decline. As a result, few studies are ever undertaken to learn what impact man's alteration of the environment has had on owls. Almost no studies have been carried out to determine how the use of agricultural chemicals affects their survival. Though Barn Owl populations seem to be stable or slightly on the upswing nationally, for example, this sociable species, so well known to the farmer, has disappeared from most of Ohio and Missouri. Spotted Owls have made the "threatened" list in Oregon, due to clear-cutting of timber. The little Western Burrowing Owl of California and its cousin the Florida Burrowing Owl, which have the amiable habit of bowing to human visitors as well as the less fortunate habit of nesting in old prairie-dog holes, have suffered tremendously from rodent-control programs aimed at poisoning ground squirrels and prairie dogs. But in most states, the only attention that owl species have received is the bureaucratic "status undetermined." It's daunting to reflect how these birds, their complex habits worked out with such artful precision over eons, can yield their place in the span of one man's lifetime, never to return for the millions of years to come.

It was once common to lose species through conscious destruction. That era faded, not with remorse for the terrible slaughter but with the rise of advanced agriculture, which made hunting superfluous, and with urbanization. Short-eared Owls have not been wiped out as pests, as Horned Owls were a few decades ago. Nor have they been shot for their feathers, nor even gunned down in significant numbers by myopic duck hunters. They are the victims only of the relentless efficiency with which we produce and consume things. The common denominator in the case of nearly every bird species in decline is the loss of habitat. Economic growth has become falsely synonymous with the consumption of plains, forests, coasts, and marshes; with the systematic simplification of the environment—the transformation of large, diverse areas into smaller, more homogeneous ones. We are losing plants and animals at a greater rate than at any time in the history of the earth. The irony of the Short-eared's decline is that one of nature's most extroverted birds of prey—a bird that practically invites our witness, our study, and affection—slips away from traditional range almost without notice. We live in a time of such tremendous distance from nature that the most magnificent creatures can disappear with nearly universal inadvertence.

There are many kinds of diversity in nature, as well as

many uses for variation. Diversity within a given species' gene pool, for instance, provides that particular species with risk insurance against disease or other calamity. Diversity of kinds in an ecological community provides stability for the entire community, a system of checks and balances. For example, during the broad sweep of the nineteenth century we exploited the Midwest prairies for agriculture, and during the twentieth century, our cities and suburbs spread into coastal wetlands. Now suppose that some time during the twenty-first century a mutant form of mouse, genetically fortified against our most powerful rodenticides, escapes from a lab and rampages over the country, wrecking crops. Had diversity been maintained, an owl invasion could bring this superabundance of rodents back into line. But there will be no owl invasion to save the farmlands, because there will not be enough owls. Then we might think bitterly of how previous generations had reduced the Short-eared Owl's habitat, and revile those who thoughtlessly squandered the variety of creation. None of this is mere supposition: it has happened before, and is happening right now. The foolish citizens of Hamelin learned long ago that if you try to cheat the Piper you can lose your own children.

As for the aesthetic loss of no longer seeing the Short-eared Owl perform its intricate courtship dance, its brilliant wounded-bird ruse, its soaring, fantastic flights; as for the loss to the poet, the philosopher, the farmer, the teacher, the psychologist, the curious child, and all those who could learn new meanings of love, freedom, devotion, and tolerance from the Bog Trotter's singing wings—this loss is beyond calculation.

# AUTUMN

## Migration Rhythms

Beholden to the hunt for nourishment, the owl is transformed in autumn from the staid homebody of Pallas Athene
to the restless wanderer of her favorite mortal, Odysseus. In
so-called rodent years, when the supply of prey is especially
abundant, owls probably travel as little as possible from their
breeding range and native nest sites, perhaps only extending
their suzerainty over a larger, cold season hunting territory,
or shifting locally to concentrate their efforts on productive
woodlots or stubble fields. But when the microtine rodent
population takes its cyclical, usually precipitous, crash, or
the signs foretell a severe winter, or a particularly successful
breeding year for owls creates the pressure of numbers, then
owls call upon the ancient avian custom of seasonal movement, which is far stronger in some owl species than in
others.

Some comparative heavyweights of the line—the Great
Horned, the Barred, and the Spotted Owl of the west—
equipped to hunt the stripped woods a.d heavily coated
against the cold, are essentially nonmigratory, as are such
owls of milder southern climes as the Florida Burrowing Owl,
the Texas Elf Owl, and the Arizona Pygmy Owl. Barn Owls,
thought to be year-round residents only fifty years ago, are
now known to participate in fall mass movements, though
not always in the north-south direction that other birds follow.

There are also the idiosyncratic movements of the northern species, such as the arctic Snowy Owl, the Boreal Owl, Hawk Owl, and the handsome, elusive Great Gray. A whole vocabulary exists to spread confusion about these strange periodic but nonannual travels, for migration usually describes only the typical yearly movement, north to south in autumn, south to north in spring. *Dispersal* indicates autumn movement, but in no set direction—for example, when Barn Owls are found flying north in September. When the northern species quite suddenly arrive in winter far south of their traditional range, the term sometimes employed is *invasion*, leaving the mistaken impression that the owls have somehow transgressed a national border and must be repulsed. Currently, the favorite word in ornithology is *incursion*, continuing the fashion of military anthropomorphism. Finally, the slightly more meaningful *irruption* describes an irregular burst of owls into nontraditional territory, though I've been unable to find out why owls "irrupt" into one place but never "erupt" out of another.

These irregular movements have been related to the rodent population cycle by examples of behavior that clearly indicate the desperate search for sustenance when semistarved owls arrive after strenuous flights. During the largest owl irruption on record, when no fewer than 13,502 Snowy Owls from the Canadian Arctic suddenly populated a belt extending from Washington State to the Atlantic seaboard in the winter of 1945-46, one Snowy Owl made a swoop at an automobile near Baranga, Michigan, and made off with a squirrel's tail adorning the car's radio antenna. A New England game warden that same winter reported that a Snowy repeatedly attacked his fur hat, and a hunter captured a Snowy after the famished owl tried to eat his leather glove.

Yet we don't know for sure whether the Snowy Owls migrate *only* according to the stress of circumstances or whether they respond to some more deep-seated rhythm: just when you think it's safe to hazard a guess, something turns theory topsy-turvy. It used to be thought that the so-called Snowy Owl invasions were triggered by the shortage of lemmings, a main article in the Snowy Owl diet. When the lemming population grows too large, they try to migrate to new territory by swimming—with no intention of committing mass suicide, as has long been falsely thought. Nevertheless, the majority of lemmings die by drowning. The Snowy Owls were thought to be forced southward during the same four-to-seven-year cycle. However, Snowy Owls have now been recorded at New York's Kennedy Airport three years in a row, casting doubt on the lemming-shortage theory. The owls seem to be coming every winter to take advantage of a population of Texas blacktail jackrabbits, which apparently escaped from a shipment to a game farm, found the airport grounds to their liking, and multiplied as only rabbits can. Thus we have the bizarre situation of an arctic owl wintering at an east-coast urban airfield to feed on southwestern rodents. Science has begun to describe where and when owls migrate, how far they fly, and under what weather conditions. But as for the cosmology of the owl's travels—of the conflict between a bird's strong instinct to remain close to its place of birth and the ancient habit of fall movement—we know amazingly little.

Of all owls, the diminutive Saw-whet Owl, *Aegolius acadicus*, Mighty Adorable of the Acadian forests, regularly makes the most fantastic voyage: a sojourn of up to fifteen hundred miles, apparently all flown at little more than ten feet off the ground. Studies show that the Saw-whets travel two distinct routes. One begins in central Ontario and extends southwest down the Ohio River Valley as far as Kentucky, branching down the Mississippi River Valley to Tennessee. The other route follows the Atlantic coastal lowlands from Maine to North Carolina. Neither flyway takes the Saw-whets across the Appalachian Mountains.

Throughout the autumn, through northeastern gales that drive the leaves before them, and under the frosty hunter's moon of November, ornithologists are out in the field to record and study the Saw-whet Owl's annual rhythm. All migrating birds employ rivers and coastlines as visual guides, or, like hawks and eagles, follow mountain ranges where updrafts create long corridors for soaring known as "movable sidewalks." Landbirds are loath to cross open water—the numerous fatalities found on shorelines after adverse winds and sudden storms are testament to the sea's perils. Indeed, one such incident in 1906, when twenty-five lifeless Acadian Owls were discovered on the shore of Lake Huron after a flash autumn storm, provided the first real evidence that Saw-whet Owls actually migrate. Thus when they reach the isthmuses, peninsulas, or points adjoining open water, the migrants congregate in vast numbers, some to rest before venturing out, some to await favorable winds or simply to procrastinate before the dangerous journey. Such concentration points, or funnels, are excellent sites for observing migratory behavior.

For two hundred years, Cape May Point, jutting off the southern New Jersey coast into Delaware Bay like a finger pointing the swarming migrants south, has been as favored an autumn stopover for ornithologists as for birds of passage on the Atlantic coast flyway. Audubon visited Cape May in the fall, though he didn't do as well as Alexander Wilson, who named two new species while rambling the Cape May meadows—Wilson's plover and the Cape May warbler. By rough timetable, the songbirds pass through Cape May in August and September in massive mixed flocks. Late September, October, and November bring raptors through by the thousands. They also arrive in rough order: the sharp-shinned and Cooper's hawks first, then kestrels and broad-wing hawks, merlins and peregrine falcons shortly thereafter with goshawks and red-tailed hawks bringing up the rear. Barn Owls are the earliest owl migrants, making their heaviest flights in late September and early October. Then in the second half of October through November, the Saw-whet migration is under way. Longeared Owls trickle through during the latter part of autumn.

The technique employed to study owl migration is the same as for all other bird species, namely, legbanding. It is an old falconer's practice, dating back to the ancient Egyptians and the desert Arabs, brought to Europe after the Crusades, and first pressed into scientific service when Johann Frisch tied strings to the legs of swallows in 1740. Due to the hard scales covering a bird's legs, a thin, lightweight alloy cylinder may be slipped on without causing injury or irritation. Each band is numbered and carries the return address of the U. S. Fish and Wildlife Service's National Banding Laboratory in Washington, which issues banding permits. Scientists, birdwatchers, hunters, and ordinary citizens who recover banded birds are requested to return the bands by mail with the date, location, and means of recovery: "Found dead" is the usual epitaph.

The banding lab's computer spins out cards once a month informing banders of all "foreign recoveries"—birds recovered away from the original banding site, not from other countries. The bander, who keeps a record of each bird at the time of banding, thus gains three bits of concrete information from each recovery: how far the bird traveled, where it went, and how long it took to get there. When a foreign recovery is made more than a year after the original banding, which is not unusual, information on the flight time is lost, but in compensation knowledge is gained about the bird's longevity. From this painstaking bookkeeping, banders can begin to piece out migration routes. What a slow, methodical procedure banders must go through to unlock only the first of migration's secret doors: only a fraction of 1 percent of all banded birds are ever recovered. Banders can spend twenty-five or fifty years in the field before claiming expertise, and many are the banders whose fathers and grandfathers banded before them, their records passed down from generation to generation like family jewels. Yet there is something appropriate about the intimate scale of this practical science, and the continuity of human generations it provides. If birdbanding is an inexact, rudimentary method, it does give naturalists the hands-on experience with birds that no radar screen or radio transmitter will ever best. More than this, banding is terrific fun.

While devotees with binoculars and spotting scopes man Cape May's hawkwatching platform, four banding stations operate from dawn to dark, drawing hawks down from the sky with live lure birds. The stations, or "blinds," are low wooden shacks with narrow open slits in the front for sighting. Out front is an arrangement of two or more springloaded bow nets, operated by trigger lines trailing along the ground back into the blind. The trapper sits inside, working the lines and watching the sky. When a hawk, circling as much as a mile high, spots the lure bird flapping, it tucks its wings under to gain velocity and commences its attack dive, which is called a "stoop." There is nothing more awesome than seeing a magnificent red-tailed hawk or peregrine falcon fold up and flash out of the sky like a bolt of feathered lightning, a vector of terrible speed and pinpoint accuracy. The trapper must keep his or her wits, carefully centering the lure bird within the circumference of the bow net, camouflaged with grasses, in order to make absolutely certain the hawk is well within the circle. A final moment of raw power and savage beauty passes as the hawk stands gorged with pride, "mantling" the prey bird with its wings, talons locked on the lure. Then the trapper pulls the trigger, the spring snaps, and the hawk is snared. It is quickly banded and released, unharmed, though anyone who has seen the way a trapped hawk gapes—its mouth wide open in angry defiance—will judge that a trapped hawk suffers a short-term indignity.

Because they are night hunters, owls cannot be actively trapped like the diurnal birds of prey: the risk of the snapping bow net injuring an improperly centered owl in the dark is simply too great. It's a shame, because every owler yearns to observe exactly how owls attack their prey. Nevertheless, alternative types of traps have to be used. The main one is a simple mist net, made of fine 61 mm. nylon mesh strung in four layers, or panels, each 12 meters long and 2.6 meters high, stretched between aluminum poles much like volley-ball nets. Each layer has a basin, or bag, at the bottom. The unwitting owl hits the net and rolls down into the bag, where it gets caught in the mesh. Some thirty mist nets are arrayed over Cape May Point in varied settings that have been found by trial and error to be most productive in the fifteen years that owl banding has taken place there. Eleven nets are stretched end to end along the western edge of North Field, a lima-bean field in growing season, stubble in autumn. The North Field nets are about ten feet from where an adjacent woodlot begins, so when owls roosting in the trees emerge to hunt the field they are immediately netted, before they have time to sense ambush. They are also coaxed to the nets by a tape loop imitating the Saw-whet's metallic whistle, or by the bander "squeaking."

Five more mist nets are slung near South Station, a small clearing between the end of the woodlot and the beginning

of Cape May marsh—a good spot because of the mixed habitat and the protected nature of the clearing itself. Six more
nets are opened in the salt hay beyond South Station, on
the speculation that the *Spartina* is excellent *Microtus* cover,
therefore attractive to owls. The remaining seven nets are
placed in the phragmites, one group of three nets in a tiny
"pocket" of the marsh, and the final four designed in a trap-
ezoid in the deep marsh, reached only by slogging through
knee-deep mud. These last are known as the "far" nets.

The logistical difficulties of surveying migratory owls are
daunting. For one thing, the nests whisper in wind gusts,
alerting the highly sensitive owls. When the moon is bright,
owls may be able to see the nets as well. Nothing prevents
a canny owl from simply redirecting its trajectory and slipping over the nets. Since no one knows exactly how migrating owls make use of unfamiliar territory, there is a large
element of guesswork involved in the arrangement of nets.
In the sense that mist nets miss what goes on above and
around them, they have been called highly "restricted eyes."
But more than twelve hundred owls have been banded at
Cape May, so the banders must be doing something right.

When an owl is disentangled from the nets, the bander
holds it firmly, but not harshly, with one hand around the
legs at the base of the body to avoid getting "footed" by the
owl's talons and the other hand around the wings to prevent
flapping and possible wing sprains. In this position, most
owls stay somewhere on a spectrum from slightly nervous
to placid or relaxed, but they are usually watchful and sometimes curious. The bird is carried in this manner to the nearest banding station and slipped head first into a cylindrical
sleeve, usually fashioned from a juice or fruit can, where it
cannot injure itself by flailing. Now the owl is ready for processing.

The holding sleeve is placed on a counterweight scale for weighing. Next, the bird is removed from the sleeve for "aging" and "sexing." Aging of Saw-whet Owls is done by inspecting the underside of the wing feathers. If the primary and secondary flight feathers show completion of adult molt, indicated by (1) a darker color with a pinkish wash, (2) wear and tear, and (3) remiges of both lighter and darker color, evincing nonsimultaneous change, then the bird is marked down as AHY—that is, After Hatching Year, or adult. Uniform plumage and lack of a rosy tinge indicate an HY, or Hatching Year, bird. For "sexing" the owl's wing is stretched along a tabletop ruler to measure the wing chord—the distance from the shoulder or carpal joint to the tip of the longest primary feather. Following the rule of sexual dimorphism that females are larger than males, Saw-whet Owls with wing chords of 134 mm. or less are determined to be male. Those with wing chords 140 mm. or more are marked female. Those in between remain undetermined. Finally, the owl is encased once more, with one leg drawn out of the holding sleeve, to receive the ring that weds the owl to ornithological history. It is a brief, unromantic ceremony. A metal leg gauge is fitted snugly over the feathered tarsus to determine the correct band size. The alloy band itself is slipped on by hand and tightened with needle-nose pliers.

Then it's farewell: the larger Barn and Long-eared owls are released from the hand holding their legs with a gentle toss upward. The smaller Saw-whet is perched on the open palm, where it sometimes remains as much as half a minute before flapping off. You feel the warm pulse of life throbbing in your hand, as the Mighty Adorable rouses its feathers and cocks it head. You experience a tremendous thrill holding this tiny bird of prey, small as a robin yet utterly magisterial.

Checking the nets is an all-night business, for the owls

cannot be left dangling and flapping in the mesh. That would tangle them further, making release much more difficult. Unfurled at dusk, the mist nets are checked every two hours until daybreak, when they must be hastily closed to prevent songbirds from getting caught as they scramble out at first light. But birds are such voracious and eager breakfast eaters that some passerines inevitably get caught. On good flight nights, when there are owls in the nets requiring release and processing, the checks can dovetail, leaving no time for an owl nap between checks. Closing is usually the longest check: the coldest hour is just before dawn. But when the last owl has flown off to roost, you hear the haunting liquid song of the Carolina wren. Standing at the edge of the meadows, you see the phragmites in sullen silhouette, the deep pinks of the dawn sky radiate over the Point, the morning clouds race up and away from the rising sun. The first sharp-shinned hawk swoops out of nowhere and is just as quickly gone. Then the immense flocks of migrants are moving, moving who knows where, and the chill air fills with a thousand flight calls—innocent, frightened, contentious, courageous—the great chorus of autumn migration.

During my first days at Cape May, everyone talked about the weather and wished they could do something about it. A high-pressure system clamped down on the Northeast, bringing the calm, bright, balmy days of Indian summer—pleasant for humans but probably confusing to migrating birds. Lacking cold temperatures and tail winds, the raptor migration entered a state of suspended animation. At the end of perfect Indian summer days in November, the rising moon and sinking sun faced off at opposite ends of the Point. The sun flattened to an oval, then separated into stripes of magenta, vermilion, and lemon, before finally submitting. Completely absent were the dramatic swirls of wintry clouds. At night the moonlight showered the woods and fields impossibly bright, so luminous that all through the night confused songbirds broke out in vestigial verses of their spring lovesongs.

Owls are said not to make migration flights under a full moon, perhaps because of the danger of being caught by other predators. Or is it because the bright moonlight obscures the stars, which birds use for compasses? We went through the motions of checking the mist nets every three hours, every night, without result. Then early one evening, just as I was waking up for the long night of checks ahead, Kate Duffy, who holds a master banding permit and heads the Cape May Owl Banding Project, called upstairs, "Can you come down? I've brought someone I want you to meet."

It was a beautiful little Saw-whet Owl, which had been so

eager it hit the bottom panel of the North Field nets even
before Katy had finished opening them—the owl was still
running in the bag when she reached it. She held the little
fellow by the feet, and the owl stared around the brightly lit
kitchen with subdued curiosity, not clicking its mandible, as
owls do when they're angry or frightened, nor flapping its
wings. I had quite forgotten, chasing the more powerful
owls of spring and summer, just how charming and appealing
this smaller owl can be. Katy gently scratched the Saw-whet
behind the head, which seemed to have a tranquilizing effect. Apparently, she said, mother owls nuzzle their nestlings
in the same spot, and when humans do it, the owl is reminded of the home nest, making it feel calm and comfortable.

Katy transferred the owl to me while she changed into
sneakers to go down to North Station to release the bird.
For five minutes I had a rare chance to admire the Mighty
Adorable's plumage and form. The Saw-whet Owl has no
ear tufts, so its crown has a smooth, sleek, sculpted shape,
olive gray speckled with delicate white spots. Its rather dainty
facial disks and white eyebrows make the amber eyes all the
more prominent—they protrude from the heavily flecked
plumage like melons in a flower garden. The white dotting
repeats all down the outermost vertical edge of the flight
feathers, so when the Saw-whet is at rest, its wings folded,
it appears to be wearing a finely polka-dotted, hooded cape
down to the tail coverts, where the speckles end in paler
white bands tipping the tail feathers. The breast and under-
parts have a background of pale buff, irregularly barred
vertically with dark chestnut, while the leg feathers are
purer buff, ending in the sharp and shiny, tiny black
talons.

The owl was such a perfect little gentleman to stand for

close inspection, I couldn't help but reach out and stroke the captive. The extreme softness of its plumage was enchanting, and when Katy came back into the room she smiled and said something that was to furnish the subject for many subsequent conversations: "It's impossible to hold a Saw-whet Owl without stroking and petting it. I've handled a lot of different birds, but there's definitely something special about Saw-whet Owls. When I was banding up at Island Beach, New Jersey, a few years back, everyone I met up there would get incredibly excited when I told them I was working with Saw-whet Owls. They all wanted to hold one—the local kids, even the guards at the State Park. Saw-whets are just softer and nicer feeling than any toy ever made. Shall we go release him?"

We walked along the dark country road that runs between the house and North field, about half a mile away. The owl hadn't been processed yet, and Katy explained that she always releases owls near the point of capture to minimize human intervention and reduce possible disorientation. At North Station, she confirmed by inspecting the plumage that this was a hatching year male on his first migration, but when she brushed back the tarsus feathers to fit the band, we had a delightful surprise: this was a reunion. The owl already wore one of Katy's bands on its leg. Checking her records, she found that it was only five days since the Mighty Adorable had been previously netted. In the meantime, he had put on seven grams in weight, now weighing ninety-five grams in all. We speculated that the summery weather might have kept the owl in the vicinity, hunting without much competition from newcomers. Perhaps he was considering going no farther south, settling in to winter in the woodlots and fields of Cape May. I was assigned the privilege of releasing him on the dirt track behind the station, where there was plenty of thick cover for an owl to recover in. I perched him on my open palm, but at the exact same instant that I removed my left hand from his legs, the owl whooshed off and proceeded with its characteristic flapping, undulating flight, closely resembling the woodcock's flight. He set down on a bare branch twenty-five feet away and immediately started head-bobbing and rotating, probably to regain his bearings, though it's possible the capture had stimulated his appetite and he was already listening for the footfall of prey.

Densely packed stars, a full moon in a necklace of cotton haze, a feeble easterly breeze, made for conditions not associated with strong migratory flights. Walking back to the house again, Katy Duffy and I talked about the goals of the autumn owl-banding project. Katy cited three major goals. The first is to "document" migration through Cape May. This has a number of meanings beyond the actual count of owls in passage. She wants to know the dates when the different species fly, and at what hours of night. In addition, she is trying to find out when hatching year and adult owls migrate—do the young birds arrive before their elders, indicating a stronger attachment to nesting territory by the adult birds?—as well as when males and females migrate in relation to each other. Also coming under the broad category of documentation, she said, are the owls' local flight patterns, how productive one set of nets is compared to the others. This ought to yield some insight into whether migrating owls avoid the phragmites, which here as elsewhere are taking over the marshes, and whether they use the open meadows, which the national habitat-saving organization known as the Nature Conservancy recently purchased as a wildlife sanctuary.

Next, the weather: Katy is hoping to learn how weather conditions affect owl migration. She has, among the few possessions of a "professional raptor bum," as she humorously refers to herself, the other studies of weather conditions and owl migration, which she offered to share with me. But, she warned, "Just because the winds and fronts affect Saw-whet Owls one way in Duluth, Minnesota, doesn't necessarily mean they do the same to Saw-whets in New Jersey."

Finally, and perhaps the most significant part of the project, are the recoveries of banded owls. This theme, the crux of any migration study, is enough to awake the double agent in Kate Duffy. When she recovers someone else's banded owl in her nets, there's positive proof of the bird's having covered so much distance. Foreign recoveries are sufficiently exciting that she sometimes jumps the gun on the Bird Banding Lab and telephones owl banders farther north—there are few enough people working in the arcane field of owl banding that they know one another. The big payoff will come when her own banded birds are recovered, but so far, in her two seasons directing the owl-banding project, the results have been scanty. One Barn Owl she banded was found later that same winter near Lancaster, Pennsylvania, about a hundred miles from Cape May but in a northwest direction. A hatching-year Saw-whet she banded was picked up as a road-kill in North Cape May, five miles north of the banding station and five days after banding, though Katy didn't find out about the recovery until she received her computer card six months later. She could only speculate as to why the bird hadn't continued south. Perhaps, she thought, it had reached the end of the peninsula and doubled back, dissuaded by the dangerous expanse of Delaware Bay, or searching for a land route skirting open water.

Even an owl as familiar as the Saw-whet is not without its private life, and migration brings these special behavioral characteristics to the fore. During my entire stay at Cape May, handling and seeing handled many of the Mighty Adorables, I was impressed by this species' spotless comportment record. They never struggle in the hand, hiss, or snap. More endearing still, they allow their human captors the familiarity of close inspection that few other owls would tolerate without angry remonstrance. I was reminded that this tameness is not only restricted to Saw-whets on migration. Two or three times during the winter I've closely approached roosting Saw-whets during daylight, once coming close enough to reach out and touch the napping bird. It calmly swiveled its head, stared for a moment, then tucked its beak back under its wings and promptly returned to sleep. Summertime campers have reported that Saw-whets will fly in to perch above the campfire, as though to say, "Hi, I live down the way in a flicker hole, and just thought I'd drop by to say hello."

Although tame with people, the Saw-whet Owl is not so in the wild. According to the American raptor specialist of the late nineteenth century, Major Charles Bendire, the Saw-whet's "a powerful, savage little fellow," who will eat twice his own weight in a single day. Small birds fear the Saw-whet to such an extent that when they discover the owl in their vicinity, they harass it mercilessly. As a result, the Saw-whet must keep extremely well hidden and immobile during the daylight hours if it is to get any rest. This forceful fear reaction to the diminutive predator has a certain mythological significance, since it was long thought in Europe that the reason small birds mobbed owls was because the owls were wicked. But nowadays, anyone working with Saw-whet Owls will tell you how magnetically popular they are. Children with no prior experience with birds, other than storybooks and television, immediately take to them and consider them beautiful, friendly, and wise. The Saw-whet, darling of the owls, has gained something of a reputation as a bird of good luck.

The owl's popular image has changed—almost no one nowadays sees doom or evil in the owl. The argument still simmers over the behavioral significance of the Saw-whet's manifest gentleness toward man. Is this curiosity about humans an indication of higher avian intelligence? Or should we interpret the Saw-whet's passivity in the hand as a sign of relative stupidity—compared, say, to the crow, which can read a hunting license at five hundred yards? It seems to me that there is a third possibility. The Saw-whet Owl is native to the deep, unpopulated Canadian forests, where contacts with humans must be negligible. Having had no previous experience with man, the migrating owl is simply unaware of any danger.

One night in early November, gusting easterly winds made us consider the relation of weather conditions to Saw-whet migration. The winds were kicking across North Field so hard that songbirds roosting for the night in the woods were being swept off their perches, landing smack in the nets. The moon had an irregular chunk taken out of its side, as if smashed with a sledge, but was otherwise brilliant and marble white. By the midnight check, Kate Duffy cried above the roar, "Let's close them up. I've never had any luck with Saw-whets on a night as windy as this."

It took us another two hours to clear the nets of sparrows,

thrushes, robins and snagged sticks and twigs, all blown in by the gusting winds. Later, warming ourselves with hot chocolate back at the house, we reviewed what's known about the weather through which Saw-whets make their migratory flights.

It seems certain that Saw-whet migration reaches a peak after the passage of each late autumn cold front that is followed by northwest winds. Hawks traveling the Atlantic coast flyway also rely on northwesterlies, or tailwinds, to push them along a southeast course. Saw-whet migration can also be correlated with phases of the moon. Flights peak during the new moon and diminish as the moon approaches full phase. This is also the pattern of nocturnally migrating passerine species and is thought to have some relation to the way birds use star constellations for direction. The unusual thing about Saw-whet migration is that neither wind direction nor moon phase is the major variable; it's wind velocity. Saw-whet Owls have a distinct tendency not to fly when strong or gusting winds blow from any direction. This is in direct contrast to the migration of other raptors, which use strong winds to speed their journey.

David Evans, the Minnesota researcher who first documented this negative correlation between gusting winds and Saw-whet migration, has proposed that something in the Saw-whet's development as a species makes it disadvantageous for them to fly in high winds. In an evolutionary sense, Evans said, Saw-whets may have sought out sheltered habitats during windy conditions to maximize hunting success. In protected clearings, Saw-whets can hear prey moving on the ground more clearly. Sharp-shinned hawks, harriers, and Short-eared Owls, to name only a few other birds of prey, have evolved wing structures more adapted to successful flight through strong winds. Saw-whet Owls, with no need to hunt in high winds, developed a wing structure more appropriate to short, rapid movements in calmer clearings. Thus when songbirds bigger than the Saw-whet Owl are getting blown off their roosts bodily, any attempt by the Saw-whet to move would be very precarious indeed. When the winds are up, and the moonlight is bright, the Saw-whet Owl lies low.

# F O U R

Whenever migration conditions are good—northwesterly breezes following passage of a cold front, with little moonshine—we listen closely for the bizarre sound that tells us a heavy owl flight is under way. This comes from the Barn Owls passing overhead just after dark. They put out an all-points bulletin that is not only unique but also nearly impossible to describe. For nights on end I've been trying to think of the right word, discarding each candidate as woefully inadequate. The Barn Owl's migration call is briefer than a shriek, less shrill than a scream. It's higher pitched than a snore or hiss. It's more sibilant than a rasp or groan, but less so than a bleat. It lacks the affirmation of a bark, the repetition of a cackle, the melancholy evenness of a hoot. Yet it's a little of each of these.

Many birds of passage make familiar flight calls on migration, but among the fowl and passerines the motive is fairly obvious: to maintain contact with fellow migrants of the same kind and keep the flock together for safety. Barn Owls aren't known to flock in migration. So what, exactly, are they doing, apart from scaring the daylights out of honest ground dwellers below? This is the sort of question most ornithologists will walk a mile through catbriers to avoid. Meanwhile, I'm developing a deep affection for the Barn or Monkey-faced Owl—for its ability to survive the toxic waste dumps, for its eccentric behavior, and especially for the way it refuses to yield hard data to man's prying science. I see white wings rush past the Cape May Point Lighthouse and think: we know almost nothing about this species—perhaps it is a ghost, after all.

Despite the Barn Owl's truly enormous range, which stretches from southern Canada all the way to Tierra del Fuego, autumn movements seem not to be uniform over the bird's home zone. In the United States, researchers have chosen 35 degrees north latitude as a kind of Barn Owl Line, dividing migratory behavior. This arbitrary division runs approximately through Fayetteville, North Carolina, and Chattanooga, Tennessee, in the east; through Little Rock, Arkansas, Oklahoma City, Oklahoma, and the Texas panhandle; to Albuquerque, New Mexico, Flagstaff, Arizona, and Bakersfield, California, in the west. Below 35 degrees, the Barn Owl shows a distinct tendency to stay home and not migrate at all, and few *Tytos* are recovered more than ninety miles from their hatching places. Moving north, just above 35 degrees, you find the most "normal" migratory Barn Owls, some of which make north—south flights of magnificent distance. The old record seems to have been held by a young Monkey-faced Owl out of Leetonia, Ohio, banded in May 1933 and recovered at the end of January 1934 in Naples, Florida, 1,075 miles away. A new record was reported by Leonard Soucy, legendary Barn Owl man of New Jersey, who has banded over five hundred Barn Owl nestlings. One nestling Soucy banded at Griggstown, New Jersey, on May 18, 1976, was recovered on November 6, 1976, in Alabama Port, Alabama, eleven hundred miles away. Soucy had another eleven-hundred-miler recovered on Sanibel Island, Florida, in 1977, but since this was a two-year-old bird there's no way of knowing if it made its trip all at once or in stages.

Almost all autumn movement takes place among the

northern range Barn Owls above 35 degrees north, but here comes the peculiarity. Around 40 percent of the recovered Barn Owls that originated north of the Barn Owl Line have never migrated south of 35 degrees. They've gone north, like another of Soucy's birds, banded in New Jersey and recovered in Massachusetts. Or, east. Or even west, the way Katy Duffy's foreign recovery traveled from Cape May to Lancaster, Pennsylvania. And the farther north in the range they live, the less inclined Barn Owls seem to move south. Except, that is, in California, where all Barn Owls recovered so far have moved south. There is scanty evidence concerning northward migration, but in Europe one study showed that young Barn Owls disperse in all directions, then settle down to nest and don't move again—a one-way, one-time journey, with no return flight. It could be that the same thing takes place among our northern-range Barn Owls. In which case this odd habit of flying north is not really migration at all but rather an extending of the Barn Owl's range northward. There is abundant evidence that as northern forests have fallen to the farmer and the developer, Barn Owls have moved in. There is also evidence that many of these pioneer Barn Owls freeze to death in cold winters on the Barn Owl frontier. The average life expectancy of southern-range Barn Owls has been found to be two years, two months, and twenty-six days. Northern-range Barn Owls have a life expectancy of only one year, one month, four days. The oldest Barn Owl on record, by the way, was the Sage of Escondido, California, world traveler, accomplished small-game hunter, author of many horrible and grotesque cries, who gave up the ghost after eleven years, six months, and four days of life.

This complex map of Barn Owl movements is further complicated by the Barn Owl's equally eccentric nesting habits. South of the Barn Owl Line, *Tyto alba* shows a fairly tidy, well-defined breeding season, which conforms to most other raptors, taking place in April, May, and June. The anomalies, once more, begin at the 35 degrees north line. Old Major Bendire reported instances of Barn Owls nesting in Washington, D.C., in December and January. By 1948, one compiler of records had gathered information showing that northern-range Barn Owls nest every month of the year, with the exception of February. Barn Owls have been found to mate and nest at a tender age—one child bride incubating eggs was captured ten months and nine days after she herself had been banded as a nestling. They also are clearly capable of double-brooding—that is, of immediately following a first nesting with a second. Since each brood can contain as many as eleven to thirteen eggs, the Barn Owl may have the highest biotic potential among owls. It sometimes seems that the Barn Owls are trying to keep up with the mice in a mad population race; indeed, this has been tentatively suggested. The theory is that Barn Owls breed more or less continuously during the upside of the *Microtus* population cycle, for a period of two to three years, then level off or cease breeding entirely during periods of rodent scarcity, roughly for another two years. If so, we have Barn Owls flying off in all directions, in all seasons, some heading north to extend the range, others flying south, never to return. A final anomaly comes from data collected at Cape May, which show that, unlike all other raptors, adult Barn Owls seem to migrate earlier in the season than the immature birds.

In sum, something peculiar is going on among Barn Owls, a vaguely comprehensible process of change in distribution, migration, reproduction, and population. Limited in our understanding by time, place, light, and memory, we can only stand beneath the Milky Way, listening for the Barn Owl's "SSSSSSSS-CHHAAAAA!!!!" overhead—and call this difficult, inexplicable thing evolution.

# F I V E

At last the cold front we waited for moved through, bringing freezing temperatures and northwest winds. When we opened the nets, dusk sprang out in its true winter colors, flaming scarlet, mauve merging with gray. Widgeons whizzed for night cover overhead, making flight calls like children's rubber bathtub ducks when they are squeezed. In the marshes, bursts of woodcock, sweeping out on whistling wings, reminded us that it was hunting season. Kate Duffy went out to open the Pocket and the Far nets, and on the way back we found a Saw-whet Owl in North Field. He was a cutie, a little hatching year male, smallest of the small, acting alternately very fierce and nonchalant. With exaggerated grace, he raised one leg, threw Katy a naughty glance, and tried to foot her.

"Stop that," said Katy, who habitually talks to the owls. "We'll have you out of here in a minute, little one."

After processing and banding, we released the owl behind the blind, where he made for a nearby limb and immediately started preening his feathers, as though to get rid of the unwanted touch of the humans. We went off to dinner at a local bar in Cape May, and the topic of our dinner conversation was inevitable.

"When August comes," Kate Duffy was saying, "my fingers start itching. I get raptor withdrawal symptoms. I need to hold an owl in my hands. To hold it and play with it, and study it. It's the only thing to keep me from getting jumpy.

To see the plumage closely, especially the underside, the shadings and the subtleties, the patterns. When I started banding owls, I told people that this was the only way I could figure out to really get to know them. Birdwatchers can observe hawks or warblers, but owls can't be so easily observed. And studying nocturnal raptors close up is just about impossible. Banding is the only way I'll ever find out just how soft their feathers are, or what the adult plumage looks like compared to the juvenile plumage. The scientist in me wants to do what's never been done before, to see what hasn't been seen. But I confess, it's gone beyond that. Before I got my master banding permit, when I was assisting other banders, it began to show in my attitude toward taking measurements. Everyone else in banding hated to do the measurements and considered it the most boring part of banding. Not me. I'd volunteer to weigh and measure the birds, just to be able to hold them. I'm obsessed with handling birds."

As we talked, we kept an alert eye on the clock, wondering how many owls would be in our nets tonight and what bits of intelligence they might add to our slim knowledge of owl migration.

"God, there are so many questions still unanswered," said the ornithologist, responding to my request to list them. "To start with, we don't know their schedule, in terms of what hours they fly on migration. We haven't mapped out a precise migration route: where are they coming from before they get to Cape May, and where do they go immediately afterward? We don't know for certain yet how they use the local habitat. Do they hit the Point and turn up the Bay coast, or head out over the water? Does migration vary much from one species to another? We're a little better versed on how weather conditions and phases of the moon affect migration. But why owls don't fly under the full moon we're still not absolutely sure. And the influence of weather conditions brings up the whole question of what stimulates owl migration in the first place. Lack of food on the home range? Temperature change? A shorter period of daylight? Then come the questions of migratory behavior. At what height do owls fly? Is migration accomplished all at once or in stages? Do owls show any flocking tendency on migration? Why, for instance, do Barn Owls make those weird flight calls? And why do adult Barn Owls seem to move before young ones—is the same true for other species? I guess I could go on, but we'd better get out there for the nine o'clock check. No one has even studied Long-eared Owl migration, as far as I know. The ideal thing would be to band owls in one place for about fifty years, gather all your recovery records, and find out where they're going and what they're up to."

The moon was a mere sliver, and darkness hugged the woods. The Horned Owls hooted softly in the arbors beyond the summer homes, and a breeze rippled low over North Field, rattling relict beans inside their dry pods. It should have been an active night in the nets, but nothing appeared on the nine o'clock or midnight checks, and I snuck off for a nap, sleeping through the 3:00 A.M. check. When Katy returned to the house to fetch me before dawn, she informed me I'd missed two Saw-whets and a Barn Owl. "You snooze, you lose," she invoked the owl bander's maxim. In a minute I'd dived into my waders, and we were off for the closing.

The moon had sunk below the sea, leaving a legacy of dark and silence. At North Field we separated, Katy going to close the Far nets, I to check South Station. Every turn of the trail was familiar, each stump to avoid, every overhang of thorns. Comfortable in the oft-worked territory, I felt a journeyman of the night, proud of my ability to make my way through the pitch woods without using a flashlight. No longer having to concentrate on where my feet fell, or to worry about tripping or getting knocked out by a stray limb, I became more alert to pure sound, and long before reaching the clearing I could already hear the heavy flapping waiting for me there. I walked the nets, flicking on my flashlight, and there they were—a pair, no less, of Long-eared Owls, *Asio otus*, trapped in the bottom panel not two feet apart.

One was hanging upside down, as if performing a headstand. The other was held only by the feet and could flap quite freely. Since this was my first chance to see Long-eareds so close, I must have gone into a fair imitation of an owl stare. They were incredibly impressive creatures, with soft camel-hair-colored lores outlining the facial disks and curving apart between the eyes and beak, almost like mustaches. The immense tapered wings gave a strong impression of power, and their lemon eyes were full of cold inquisitiveness. I wanted to remain right there and look and look—only the master bander can legally remove owls from the nets. But I recalled Kate Duffy's warning that standing too close to netted birds without releasing them can frustrate them into fits of wild flapping. This might attract larger predators, fatigue the birds unnecessarily, or entangle them further. So I clicked off my flashlight and went to check the last net, strung along the bayberry and wild rose on the western edge of the station clearing. There was another Long-eared Owl trapped there, about halfway between the woods and where the marsh began, and only marginally higher than its confreres. These Long-eareds were apparently low riders, and I found myself asking out loud, "Were

you guys traveling together, or did one of you get caught
and make noise and the rest of you come in to see what was
up? Are you brothers and sisters?"

I could hear the rubbery screek of Katy's waders coming
through the woods. When she entered the clearing, I blur-
ted out, "Congratulations, you've got a three-owl night—
Saw-whet, Barn, and Long-eared."

"All right!" she cheered, looking over the situation to
decide which owl to release first. "What you always want to
do is release the easiest owl first, to reduce the total time
they spend in the mesh to a minimum," she explained. "We're
also going to have to work fast to get these guys banded and
outta here before it gets light."

While I held the flashlight, the ornithologist's nimble fingers went to work, tracing each minute loop through the
bird's feathers. Sometimes she had to blow the feathers back
to track the knot into the dense pile. She enlarged each loop
until it could be brought over the wing, or head, or around
the foot, then held it out cat's-cradle style to see where it fit
into the mass of tangle. The idea is to try to back the owl
out of the mesh the same way it went in; otherwise you run
the risk of doubling the knot over on itself, making the mess
of knots worse. Although a birdbander's patience for untan-
gling minuscule knots in freezing temperatures may be ex-
quisitely high, the owl's patience has stricter limits. As she
freed each bird, Katy handed it to me to hold. The owls
watched me with stiff reproach, ignoring each other, and
puffed out their breast feathers in an intimidation posture,
bulking themselves to look bigger and more ferocious. In
body language, they were saying, "You can look, but you'd
better not touch." In another few minutes we were bearing
our harvest of owls back to South Station for processing.

In the yellow light of the Coleman lantern, Katy Duffy

processed the first Long-eared, while, to save the time of slipping them in and out of sleeves, I stood by with a resolute, unyielding owl in each hand. In this rapturous moment for an owler, a couplet of Ted Hughes's poetry came back to me:

*Owls, owls, nothing but owls*
*The most fantastical of fowls.*

Katy Duffy was right: admiring their plumage and reactions from point-blank range, I observed details that had completely escaped notice in a year of continual, but more distant, pursuit. The ear tufts were composed of only three feathers—a large, tapered feather in front, then a small one behind, and a still smaller one behind that. They seemed to be able to erect and flatten each tuft separately, the way some people can wiggle one ear at a time. The underside of the wings had a heavy buff-to-camel-hair coloration. Against a white background, the breast feathers had distinct, neat cross-hatchings, as if a priest had dipped his finger in dark chocolate before making the sign of the cross on each feather. What wonderful complexity, with each part of the owl's body covered in its own pattern, chosen from the warm browns, the grays, the off-whites. It's been said that nature is God's art, and inspecting birds in the hand, you can't fail to believe it's true.

Katy's voice brought me out of this reverie—as usual, she was addressing an owl: "You can go by yourself, it's still dark enough for you to fly. Bye!" And she scooted out the door of the blind, releasing the banded Long-eared at the edge of the clearing. It wasted no time flapping heavily off into the pines. But even as she processed the second Long-eared, the pearl gray light of dawn seeped through the cracks in the blind's rough boards. It's not a good idea to release banded owls after daybreak, when voracious hawks are beating the brush for breakfast, and flocks of crows can gang up on a slightly disoriented owl. The ornithologist was hesitant about whether to release the second bird or "perch" it—that is, find it a roost on a branch in a dark grove to let the owl recover from the handling. Presently, Katy decided to release the second owl, but instead of winging away, the bird dropped to the ground, puffed its chest feathers out, spread its wings, and put on an intimidation display.

"Keep an eye on that one," said Katy, rushing back inside to process the last of the trio. "If he doesn't get going in another minute, we'll have to go perch him."

I turned to the observation slit at the front of the blind, and then time lost its power to separate events. The owl was still on the ground, he was up in a low bayberry bush, a sharp-shinned hawk cruised down from the blindside. I was watching in horror, then crashing out the door. The door was banging, the sharpie, spooked at the noise, shot up over the owl, and vanished into the trees. The owl was taking off for the woods, and I was back inside again. Less than ten seconds had elapsed since this rush of events began, seconds of epiphany in which I sensed for the first time how an owl's lifespan of only two, or perhaps three, years might seem quite long if all the moments were lived at such a high existential pitch. All I reported back to Kate Duffy was, "He's gone."

Katy carried the last Long-eared out, stalked through the underbrush, and, standing on tiptoes, gently deposited the bird on a branch in the pine grove. As soon as she released her hold, however, the owl flew right back out of cover, made a smooth, tight circle, and with two disdainful flaps, headed off in a float toward North Field. Typically cantankerous owl behavior, I thought, watching it disappear into the trees. Kate Duffy said, "Did you notice how they all went in the same direction? That's good. Maybe they're going to a communal roost. It's neat when there's a lot of action, isn't it?"

In the bald light of day, almost two hours after we started the final check, our labors were coming to a close. Bleary-eyed and stomachs rumbling, we still felt more exhilarated than exhausted. Perhaps we hadn't unlocked any new owl secrets, gained owl knowledge, nor penetrated the owl world. But we were staying up with the owls, traveling with the owls, and by all odds, at this moment, beginning to look like owls, too. Let friends and kinsmen worry that if we don't quit this mad pursuit we'll turn into owls—nothing would give greater pleasure than to know the owl from the inside out. Only then could we begin to pierce the owl's inner life, which the nightbird keeps well hidden from our paltry senses.

Katy went out to close the nets in the marsh pocket, while I trekked back through the woods to furl the North Field nets. On my way, at the last bend of the trail, I heard a scrumming and rustling in the trees. When I moved a few steps into the thickets, one of our Long-eareds flushed from a low branch. I admired its hulky profile, gliding serenely out over North Field. It made a turn north, followed the edge of the woods, then disappeared into heavy cover, searching for a more secluded spot to roost.

# INDEX

## About the Author

Jonathan Evan Maslow writes on natural history, politics, sports, and travel. His work has appeared in *GEO*, *The Atlantic Monthly*, *The New York Times*, and the *Boston Globe*, among other periodicals. *The Owl Papers* was his first book. His second, *Bird of Life, Bird of Death*, was nominated for the National Book Critics' Circle Award. He recently received a Guggenheim Fellowship to complete his third book. He lives in Cape May County, New Jersey.